Houghton Mifflin Harcourt

CALIFORNIA

MATH

Expressions
Common Core

Dr. Karen C. Fuson

GRADE

4

This material is based upon work supported by the
National Science Foundation
under Grant Numbers
ESI-9816320, REC-9806020, and RED-935373.

Any opinions, findings, and conclusions, or recommendations expressed in this material
are those of the author and do not necessarily reflect the views of the National Science Foundation.

CONTENTS

CONTENTS *(continued)*

Dear Family,

Your child is learning math in an innovative program called *Math Expressions*. In Unit 1, your child will use place value drawings and charts to understand that the value of each place is 10 times greater than the value of the place to its right. This understanding is essential when comparing, rounding, or adding multidigit numbers. *Math Expressions* encourages children to think about "making new groups" to help them understand place values.

We call the method below "New Groups Above". The numbers that represent the new groups are written above the problem.

1. Add the ones:

5 + 7 = 12 ones
12 = 2 ones + 10 ones,
and 10 ones = 1 new ten.

$$\begin{array}{r} \overset{1}{5,1\,7\,5} \\ +\ 3,9\,6\,7 \\ \hline 2 \end{array}$$

2. Add the tens:

1 + 7 + 6 = 14 tens
14 = 4 tens + 10 tens,
and 10 tens = 1 new hundred.

$$\begin{array}{r} \overset{1\ 1}{5,1\,7\,5} \\ +\ 3,9\,6\,7 \\ \hline 4\,2 \end{array}$$

3. Add the hundreds:

1 + 1 + 9 = 11 hundreds
11 = 1 hundred + 10 hundreds,
and 10 hundreds = 1 new thousand.

$$\begin{array}{r} \overset{1\ \ 1\ 1}{5,1\,7\,5} \\ +\ 3,9\,6\,7 \\ \hline 1\,4\,2 \end{array}$$

4. Add the thousands:

1 + 5 + 3 = 9 thousands

$$\begin{array}{r} \overset{1\ \ 1\ 1}{5,1\,7\,5} \\ +\ 3,9\,6\,7 \\ \hline 9,1\,4\,2 \end{array}$$

We call the following method "New Groups Below." The steps are the same, but the new groups are written below the addends.

1.
$$\begin{array}{r} 5,1\,7\,5 \\ +\ 3,9\,6\,7 \\ \hline {}_{1}2 \end{array}$$

2.
$$\begin{array}{r} 5,1\,7\,5 \\ +\ 3,9\,6\,7 \\ \hline {}_{1\,1}4\,2 \end{array}$$

3.
$$\begin{array}{r} 5,1\,7\,5 \\ +\ 3,9\,6\,7 \\ \hline {}_{1\,1\,1}4\,2 \end{array}$$

4.
$$\begin{array}{r} 5,1\,7\,5 \\ +\ 3,9\,6\,7 \\ \hline {}_{1\,1\,1}9,1\,4\,2 \end{array}$$

It is easier to see the totals for each column (12 and 14) and adding is easier because you add the two numbers you see and then add the 1.

It is important that your child maintains his or her home practice with basic multiplication and division.

Sincerely,
Your child's teacher

CA CC

Unit 1 addresses the following standards from the *Common Core State Standards for Mathematics with California Additions*: **4.NBT.1, 4.NBT.2, 4.NBT.3, 4.NBT.4, 4.MD.2** and all Mathematical Practices.

Un vistazo general al contenido

Estimada familia,

Su niño está aprendiendo matemáticas mediante el programa *Math Expressions*. En la Unidad 1, se usarán dibujos y tablas de valor posicional para comprender que el valor de cada lugar es 10 veces mayor que el valor del lugar a su derecha. Comprender esto es esencial para comparar, redondear o sumar números de varios dígitos. *Math Expressions* enseña a pensar en "formar grupos nuevos" para comprender los valores posicionales.

Este método se llama "Grupos nuevos arriba". Los números que representan los grupos nuevos se escriben arriba del problema:

1. Suma las unidades:

5 + 7 = 12 unidades
12 = 2 unidades + 10 unidades,
y 10 unidades = 1 nueva decena.

$$\begin{array}{r} {}^{1} \\ 5,1\ 7\ 5 \\ +\ 3,9\ 6\ 7 \\ \hline 2 \end{array}$$

2. Suma las decenas:

1 + 7 + 6 = 14 decenas
14 = 4 decenas + 10 decenas,
y 10 decenas = 1 nueva centena.

$$\begin{array}{r} {}^{1\ 1} \\ 5,1\ 7\ 5 \\ +\ 3,9\ 6\ 7 \\ \hline 4\ 2 \end{array}$$

3. Suma las centenas:

1 + 1 + 9 = 11 centenas
11 = 1 centenas + 10 centenas,
y 10 centenas = 1 nuevo millar.

$$\begin{array}{r} {}^{1\ 1\ 1} \\ 5,1\ 7\ 5 \\ +\ 3,9\ 6\ 7 \\ \hline 1\ 4\ 2 \end{array}$$

4. Suma los millares:

1 + 5 + 3 = 9 millares

$$\begin{array}{r} {}^{1\ 1\ 1} \\ 5,1\ 7\ 5 \\ +\ 3,9\ 6\ 7 \\ \hline 9,1\ 4\ 2 \end{array}$$

Este método se llama "Grupos nuevos abajo". Los pasos son iguales, pero los nuevos grupos se escriben abajo de los sumandos:

Es más fácil ver los totales de cada columna (12 y 14) y es más fácil sumar porque sumas los dos números que ves, y luego sumas 1.

1.
$$\begin{array}{r} 5,1\ 7\ 5 \\ +\ 3,9\ 6\ 7 \\ \hline 2 \end{array}$$

2.
$$\begin{array}{r} 5,1\ 7\ 5 \\ +\ 3,9\ 6\ 7 \\ \hline 4\ 2 \end{array}$$

3.
$$\begin{array}{r} 5,1\ 7\ 5 \\ +\ 3,9\ 6\ 7 \\ \hline 1\ 4\ 2 \end{array}$$

4.
$$\begin{array}{r} 5,1\ 7\ 5 \\ +\ 3,9\ 6\ 7 \\ \hline 9,1\ 4\ 2 \end{array}$$

Es importante que su niño siga practicando las multiplicaciones y divisiones básicas en casa.

Atentamente,
El maestro de su niño

CA CC

En la Unidad 1 se aplican los siguientes estándares auxiliares, contenidos en los *Estándares estatales comunes de matemáticas con adiciones para California*: **4.NBT.1, 4.NBT.2, 4.NBT.3, 4.NBT.4, 4.MD.2** y todos los de prácticas matemáticas.

► **Whole Number Secret Code Cards**

1,000	100	10	1
1,000	100	1 0	1

2,000	200	20	2
2,000	200	2 0	2

3,000	300	30	3
3,000	300	3 0	3

4,000	400	40	4
4,000	400	4 0	4

5,000	500	50	5
5,000	500	5 0	5

6,000	600	60	6
6,000	600	6 0	6

7,000	700	70	7
7,000	700	7 0	7

8,000	800	80	8
8,000	800	8 0	8

9,000	900	90	9
9,000	900	9 0	9

► Whole Number Secret Code Cards

one	ten (teen) (one ten)	one hundred	one thousand
two	twenty (two tens)	two hundred	two thousand
three	thirty (three tens)	three hundred	three thousand
four	forty (four tens)	four hundred	four thousand
five	fifty (five tens)	five hundred	five thousand
six	sixty (six tens)	six hundred	six thousand
seven	seventy (seven tens)	seven hundred	seven thousand
eight	eighty (eight tens)	eight hundred	eight thousand
nine	ninety (nine tens)	nine hundred	nine thousand

Whole Number Secret Code Cards

▶ Summarize Rounding Rules

Use these rounding frames as a visual aid when rounding
to the nearest 10, 100, 1,000.

Nearest 10	Nearest 100	Nearest 1,000
100	1,000	10,000
90	900	9,000
80	800	8,000
70	700	7,000
60	600	6,000
50	500	5,000
40	400	4,000
30	300	3,000
20	200	2,000
10	100	1,000

Round to the nearest ten.

1. 87 _____

2. 16 _____

3. 171 _____

4. 2,165 _____

5. 5,114 _____

6. 3,098 _____

Round to the nearest hundred.

7. 734 _____

8. 363 _____

9. 178 _____

10. 6,249 _____

11. 8,251 _____

12. 8,992 _____

Round to the nearest thousand.

13. 1,275 _____

14. 8,655 _____

15. 5,482 _____

16. 3,804 _____

17. 1,501 _____

18. 9,702 _____

Name _____ **Date** _____

CA CC Content Standards **4.NBT.1, 4.NBT.2**
Mathematical Practices **MP.2, MP.5, MP.7**

▶ Discuss and Summarize

Patterns to Millions

Hundred Millions	Ten Millions	Millions	Hundred Thousands	Ten Thousands	Thousands	Hundreds	Tens	Ones
100,000,000	10,000,000	1,000,000	100,000	10,000	1,000	100	10	1
millions			*thousands*			*[ones]*		

The Patterns to Millions chart shows that each digit in the number has a place value name. When we read a number, we do not say the place value name. We say the group name.

We say the word *million* after the digits in the millions group.

We say the word *thousand* after the digits in the thousands group.

We do not say the word *ones* after the digits in the ones group.

To read greater numbers, say each group of digits as if they were in the hundreds, tens, and ones places and then add the special name for that group.

▶ Read Numbers

Use your Whole Number Secret Code cards to make the groups of digits as shown below. Put them in the spaces on the Reading Millions Frame below to read them.

28,374   123,456   458,726   654,321   92,148   789,321

Reading Millions Frame

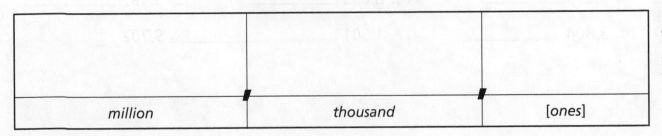

million	*thousand*	*[ones]*

Family Letter

Content Overview

Dear Family,

Your child is now learning about subtraction. A common subtraction mistake is subtracting in the wrong direction. Children may think that they always subtract the smaller digit from the larger digit, but this is not true. To help children avoid this mistake, the *Math Expressions* program encourages children to "fix" numbers first and then subtract.

$$\begin{array}{r} \cancel{1,634} \\ -\ \cancel{158} \\ \hline \cancel{1,524} \end{array}$$

When one or more digits in the top number are smaller than the corresponding digits in the bottom number, fix the numbers by "ungrouping." For example, $1,634 - 158$ is shown below:

1. We cannot subtract 8 ones from 4 ones. We get more ones by ungrouping 1 ten to make 10 ones.

We now have 14 ones and only 2 tens.

$$\begin{array}{r} {}^{2\ 14}\\ 1,6\,\cancel{3}\,\cancel{4} \\ -\ \ \ 1\,5\,8 \\ \hline \end{array}$$

2. We cannot subtract 5 tens from 2 tens. We get more tens by ungrouping 1 hundred to make 10 tens.

We now have 12 tens and only 5 hundreds.

$$\begin{array}{r} {}^{\ \ 12}\\ {}^{5\ \cancel{2}\,14}\\ 1,\cancel{6}\,\cancel{3}\,\cancel{4} \\ -\ \ \ 1\,5\,8 \\ \hline \end{array}$$

3. Now we can subtract:
$1 - 0 = 1$ thousand
$5 - 1 = 4$ hundreds
$12 - 5 = 7$ tens
$14 - 8 = 6$ ones

$$\begin{array}{r} {}^{\ \ 12}\\ {}^{5\ \cancel{2}\,14}\\ 1,\cancel{6}\,\cancel{3}\,\cancel{4} \\ -\ \ \ 1\,5\,8 \\ \hline 1,4\,7\,6 \end{array}$$

In the method above, the numbers are ungrouped from right to left, but students can also ungroup from left to right. Children can choose whichever way works best for them.

Your child should also continue to practice multiplication and division skills at home.

If you have any questions or comments, please call or write me.

Sincerely,
Your child's teacher

 CA CC

Unit 1 addresses the following standards from the *Common Core State Standards for Mathematics with California Additions:* **4.NBT.3, 4.NBT.4, 4.MD.2** and all Mathematical Practices.

Estimada familia:

Ahora su niño está aprendiendo a restar. Un error muy común al restar, es hacerlo en la dirección equivocada. Los niños pueden pensar que siempre se resta el dígito más pequeño del dígito más grande, pero no es verdad. Para ayudar a los niños a no cometer este error, el programa *Math Expressions* les propone "arreglar" los números primero y luego restar.

$$\begin{array}{r} 1{,}6\cancel{3}4 \\ -\ \ 158 \\ \hline 1{,}52\cancel{4} \end{array}$$

Cuando uno o más dígitos del número de arriba son más pequeños que los dígitos correspondientes del número de abajo, se arreglan los números "desagrupándolos". Por ejemplo, 1,634 − 158 se muestra abajo:

1. No podemos restar 8 unidades de 4 unidades. Obtenemos más unidades al desagrupar 1 decena para formar 10 unidades.

Ahora tenemos 14 unidades y solamente 2 decenas.

$$\begin{array}{r} {}^{2\ 14}\\ 1{,}6\cancel{3}\cancel{4} \\ -\ \ 158 \end{array}$$

2. No podemos restar 5 decenas de 2 decenas. Obtenemos más decenas al desagrupar 1 centena para formar 10 decenas.

Ahora tenemos 12 decenas y solamente 5 centenas.

$$\begin{array}{r} {}^{\ \ 12}\\ {}^{5\ \cancel{2}14}\\ 1{,}\cancel{6}\cancel{3}\cancel{4} \\ -\ \ 158 \end{array}$$

3. Ahora podemos restar:

1 − 0 = 1 millar
5 − 1 = 4 centenas
12 − 5 = 7 decenas
14 − 8 = 6 unidades

$$\begin{array}{r} {}^{\ \ 12}\\ {}^{5\ \cancel{2}14}\\ 1{,}\cancel{6}\cancel{3}\cancel{4} \\ -\ \ 158 \\ \hline 1{,}476 \end{array}$$

En el método de arriba se desagrupan los números de derecha a izquierda, pero también se pueden desagrupar de izquierda a derecha. Los niños pueden escoger la manera que les resulte más fácil.

Su niño también debe seguir practicando las destrezas de multiplicación y de división en casa.

Si tiene alguna pregunta, por favor comuníquese conmigo.

Atentamente,
El maestro de su niño

CA CC

En la Unidad 1 se aplican los siguientes estándares auxiliares, contenidos en los *Estándares estatales comunes de matemáticas con adiciones para California*: **4.NBT.3, 4.NBT.4, 4.MD.2** y todos los de prácticas matemáticas.

Subtract. Show your new groups.

10. 7,919
    − 3,846

11. 8,502
    − 3,749

12. 4,221
    − 2,805

13. 7,000
    − 572

14. 4,650
    − 2,793

15. 4,605
    − 1,711

16. 3,120
    −   38

17. 6,082
    −   95

18. 2,107
    − 428

19. 1,852
    − 964

20. 3,692
    − 2,704

21. 8,715
    − 6,742

22. 6,000
    − 4,351

23. 7,400
    − 1,215

24. 3,583
    − 1,794

Solve.

25. Jake has 647 pennies in his penny collection album.
The album has space for 1,000 pennies. How many
more pennies can Jake place in his album?

_____

26. A ship is making an 8,509-mile voyage. So far,
it has sailed 2,957 miles. How many miles of the
voyage remain?

_____

Name _____   **Date** _____

CA CC Content Standards **4.NBT.3, 4.NBT.4**
Mathematical Practices **MP.1, MP.4**

▶ Math and Bridges

Bridges are structures that are built to get over obstacles like water, a valley, or roads. Bridges can be made of concrete, steel, or even tree roots. Engineers and designers do a lot of math to be sure a bridge will stand up to its use and the forces of nature that affect it.

Lengths of Bridges		
Bridge	**Length Over Water (ft)**	
Manchac Swamp Bridge, U.S.A.	121,440	
Hangzhou Bay Bridge, China	117,057	
Lake Pontchartrain Causeway, U.S.A.	125,664	
Jiaozhou Bay Bridge, China	139,392	

1. Use the data in the table above to make a bar graph.

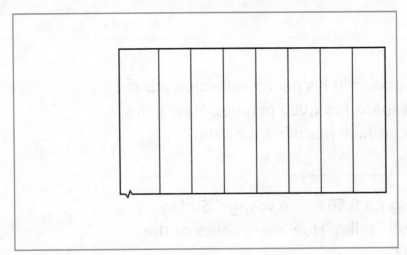

Name

Date

1. Anthony's family drives 659 miles from Miami to Atlanta. Then they drive another 247 miles to Nashville. How far does Anthony's family drive in all? Show your work.

2. A scientist measures 3,470 milliliters of water into a beaker. She pours 2,518 milliliters of the water in a solution. If the beaker can hold 5,000 milliliters, how much water is needed to fill the beaker? Show your work. Then show a way to check your answer.

3. Fill in the blank to show the number of hundreds.

4,500 = _____ hundreds

Explain how you know.

4. A mining truck is loaded with 147,265 kilograms of dirt. Another 129,416 kilograms of dirt is added. What is the total mass of the dirt in the mining truck? Show your work.

5. The downtown location of Mike's Bikes earned $179,456 last year. The store's riverside location earned $145,690. The store with the greater earnings gets an award. Which store gets the award? Show your work.

6. Select another form of 65,042. Mark all that apply.

Ⓐ 6 + 5 + 0 + 4 + 2

Ⓑ sixty-five thousand, forty-two

Ⓒ 60,000 + 5,000 + 40 + 2

Ⓓ six hundred fifty, forty-two

7. For numbers 7a–7e, choose Yes or No to tell if the
   number is rounded to the nearest thousand.

   7a. 234,566
       235,000   ○ Yes   ○ No

   7b. 7,893
       7,900   ○ Yes   ○ No

   7c. 64,498
       65,000   ○ Yes   ○ No

   7d. 958,075
       958,000   ○ Yes   ○ No

   7e. 49,826
       50,000   ○ Yes   ○ No

8. For numbers 8a–8e, choose True or False to describe
   the statement.

   8a. 34,639 > 34,369   ○ True   ○ False

   8b. 2,709 = 2,790   ○ True   ○ False

   8c. 480,920 > 480,902   ○ True   ○ False

   8d. 259 < 261   ○ True   ○ False

   8e. 6,924 < 6,299   ○ True   ○ False

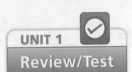
9. Make a place value drawing for 1,534.

[blank box]

10. For numbers 10a–10e, write 685,203 rounded to the nearest place value.

10a. ten _____

10b. hundred _____

10c. thousand _____

10d. ten thousand _____

10e. hundred thousand _____

11. For numbers 11a–11d, find the sum or difference.

11a.   4,379
     + 3,284

11c.   389,416
     + 237,825

11b.   57,340
     − 26,817

11d.   648,939
     − 584,172

12. There were 2,683 books sold at a bookstore this year. There were 1,317 more books sold last year. How many books were sold last year? Write an equation for the problem then solve it. Show your work.

13. Wren added the numbers 1,376 and 6,275.

Part A

Write the addends and the sum in the break-apart drawing. Then complete the two addition problems represented by the break-apart drawing.

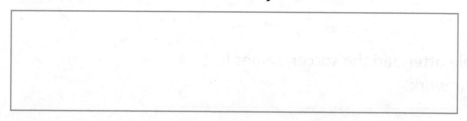

Part B

Write a word problem that requires subtracting 1,376 from 7,651.

14. Last week there were two soccer games. There were 3,982 people at the first soccer game. There were 1,886 fewer people at the second soccer game than at the first soccer game.

Part A

How many people attended the soccer games last week? Show your work.

Part B

Explain how you found your answer.

15. Order the numbers from least to greatest by writing a number in each box.

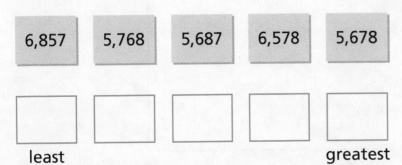

6,857   5,768   5,687   6,578   5,678

least   greatest

Family Letter

Content Overview

Dear Family,

In this unit, your child will be learning about the common multiplication method that most adults know. However, they will also explore ways to draw multiplication. *Math Expressions* uses area of rectangles to show multiplication.

	30	+	7
20	20 × 30 = 600		20 × 7 = 140
+			
4	4 × 30 = 120		4 × 7 = 28

Area Method:

$$20 \times 30 = 600$$
$$20 \times 7 = 140$$
$$4 \times 30 = 120$$
$$4 \times 7 = 28$$
$$\text{Total} = 888$$

Shortcut Method:

$$\overset{\overset{1}{2}}{37}$$
$$\times\ 24$$
$$\overline{148}$$
$$74$$
$$\overline{888}$$

Area drawings help all students see multiplication. They also help students remember what numbers they need to multiply and what numbers make up the total.

Your child will also learn to find products involving single-digit numbers, tens, and hundreds by factoring the tens or hundreds. For example,

$$200 \times 30 = 2 \times 100 \times 3 \times 10$$
$$= 2 \times 3 \times 100 \times 10$$
$$= 6 \times 1{,}000 = 6{,}000$$

By observing the zeros patterns in products like these, your child will learn to do such multiplications mentally.

If your child is still not confident with single-digit multiplication and division, we urge you to set aside a few minutes every night for multiplication and division practice. In a few more weeks, the class will be doing multidigit division, so it is very important that your child be both fast and accurate with basic multiplication and division.

If you need practice materials, please contact me.

Sincerely,
Your child's teacher

CA CC

Unit 2 addresses the following standards from the *Common Core State Standards for Mathematics with California Additions*: **4.OA.3, 4.NBT.1, 4.NBT.2, 4.NBT.3, 4.NBT.5, 4.MD.2** and all Mathematical Practices.

Un vistazo general al contenido

Estimada familia:

En esta unidad, su niño estará aprendiendo el método de multiplicación común que la mayoría de los adultos conoce. Sin embargo, también explorará maneras de dibujar la multiplicación. Para mostrar la multiplicación, *Math Expressions* usa el método del área del rectángulo.

	30	+	7
20	20 × 30 = 600		20 × 7 = 140
+			
4	4 × 30 = 120		4 × 7 = 28

Método del área

$$20 \times 30 = 600$$
$$20 \times 7 = 140$$
$$4 \times 30 = 120$$
$$4 \times 7 = 28$$
Total = 888

Método más corto

$$\begin{array}{r} {}^{1}_{2} \\ 37 \\ \times\ 24 \\ \hline 148 \\ 74 \\ \hline 888 \end{array}$$

Los dibujos de área ayudan a los estudiantes a visualizar la multiplicación. También los ayuda a recordar cuáles números tienen que multiplicar y cuáles números forman el total.

Su niño también aprenderá a hallar productos relacionados con números de un solo dígito, con decenas y con centenas, factorizando las decenas o las centenas. Por ejemplo:

$$200 \times 30 = 2 \times 100 \times 3 \times 10$$
$$= 2 \times 3 \times 100 \times 10$$
$$= 6 \times 1{,}000 = 6{,}000$$

Al observar los patrones de ceros en productos como estos, su niño aprenderá a hacer dichas multiplicaciones mentalmente.

Si su niño todavía no domina la multiplicación y la división con números de un solo dígito, le sugerimos que dedique algunos minutos todas las noches para practicar la multiplicación y la división. Dentro de pocas semanas, la clase hará divisiones con números de varios dígitos, por eso es muy importante que su niño haga las operaciones básicas de multiplicación y de división de manera rápida y exacta.

Si necesita materiales para practicar, comuníquese conmigo.

Atentamente,
El maestro de su niño

CA CC

En la Unidad 2 se aplican los siguientes estándares auxiliares, contendidos en los *Estándares estatales comunes de matemáticas con adiciones para California*: **4.OA.3, 4.NBT.1, 4.NBT.2, 4.NBT.3, 4.NBT.5, 4.MD.2** y todos los de prácticas matemáticas.

Arrays and Area Models

▶ Model a Product of Tens

Olivia wants to tile the top of a table. The table is 20 inches by 30 inches. Olivia needs to find the area of the table in square inches.

2. Find the area of this 20 × 30 rectangle by dividing it into 10-by-10 squares of 100.

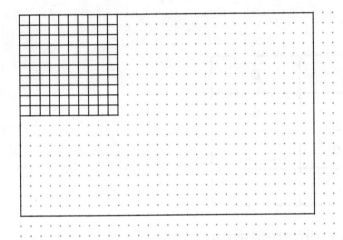

3. Each tile is a 1-inch square. How many tiles does Olivia need to cover the tabletop? _____

4. Each box of tiles contains 100 tiles. How many boxes of tiles does Olivia need to buy? _____

▶ Factor the Tens

5. Complete the steps to show your work in Exercise 2 numerically.

$20 \times 30 = ($ _____ $\times 10) \times ($ _____ $\times 10)$

$\qquad = ($ _____ $\times$ _____ $) \times (10 \times 10)$

$\qquad =$ _____ $\times 100$

$\qquad = 600$

6. Is it true that 20 × 30 = 30 × 20? Explain how you know.

_____

CA CC Content Standards **4.NBT.1, 4.NBT.5**
Mathematical Practices **MP.1, MP.6, MP.8**

Name _____ **Date** _____

▶ Look for Patterns

Multiplying greater numbers in your head is easier when you learn patterns of multiplication with tens.

Start with column A and look for the patterns used to get the expressions in each column. Copy and complete the table.

Table 1

	A	B	C	D
	2 × 3	2 × 1 × 3 × 1	6 × 1	6
1.	2 × 30	2 × 1 × 3 × 10	6 × 10	_____
2.	20 × 30	2 × 10 × 3 × 10	_____	_____

3. How are the expressions in column B different from the expressions in column A?

_____

_____

4. In column C, we see that each expression can be written as a number times a place value. Which of these **factors** gives more information about the size of the **product**?

_____

5. Why is 6 the first digit of the products in column D?

_____

6. Why are there different numbers of zeros in the products in column D?

_____

_____

► **Compare Tables**

Copy and complete each table.

Table 2

	A	B	C	D
	6 × 3	6 × 1 × 3 × 1	18 × 1	18
7.	6 × 30	6 × 1 × 3 × 10	18 × 10	_____
8.	60 × 30	6 × 10 × 3 × 10	_____	_____

Table 3

	A	B	C	D
	5 × 8	5 × 1 × 8 × 1	40 × 1	40
9.	5 × 80	5 × 1 × 8 × 10	40 × 10	_____
10.	50 × 80	_____	_____	_____

11. Why do the products in Table 2 have more digits than the products in Table 1?

_____

_____

12. Why are there more zeros in the products in Table 3 than the products in Table 2?

_____

_____

▶ **Explore the Area Model**

	20	+	6

4

1. How many square units of area are there in the tens part of the drawing? _____

2. What multiplication equation gives the area of the tens part of the drawing? Write this equation in its rectangle.

   _____

3. How many square units of area are there in the ones part? _____

4. What multiplication equation gives the area of the ones part? Write this equation in its rectangle. _____

5. What is the total of the two areas? _____

6. How do you know that 104 is the correct product of 4 × 26?

   _____

7. Read problems A and B.

   A. Al's photo album has 26 pages. Each page has 4 photos. How many photos are in Al's album?

   B. Nick took 4 photos. Henri took 26 photos. How many more photos did Henri take than Nick?

   Which problem could you solve using the multiplication you just did? Explain why.

   _____

   _____

   _____

Model One-Digit by Two-Digit Multiplication

CA CC Content Standards **4.NBT.5**
Mathematical Practices **MP.1, MP.2, MP.4**

Name _____ **Date** _____

VOCABULARY
Place Value Sections Method

▶ **Use the Place Value Sections Method**

You can use an area model to demonstrate the
Place Value Sections Method. This strategy is
used below for multiplying a one-digit number
by a two-digit number.

Complete the steps.

27 =   20   +   7

| 5 | 5 × 20 = 100 | 5 × 7 = 35 |

5   + _____

**Use the Place Value Sections Method to solve the problem.
Complete the steps.**

1. The fourth-grade class is participating in a walk-a-thon.
   Each student will walk 8 laps around the track. There
   are 92 fourth-grade students. How many laps will the
   fourth-grade class walk?

   _____

   92 =   90   +   2

   | 8 | ___ × ___ = ___ | ___ × ___ = ___ |

   8   + _____

**Draw an area model and use the Place Value Sections
Method to solve the problem.**

2. A football coach is ordering 3 shirts for each football player.
   There are 54 players in the football program. How many
   shirts does the coach need to order for the entire program?

   _____

VOCABULARY
Expanded Notation Method

▶ Use the Expanded Notation Method

You can also use an area model to show how to use the **Expanded Notation Method**. Use the Expanded Notation Method to solve 5 × 27 below.

Complete the steps.

3.
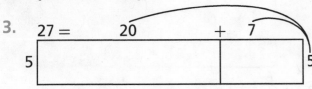

$$27 = \_\_\_ + \_\_\_$$
$$\times 5 = \_\_\_$$
$$\_\_\_ \times \_\_\_ = \_\_\_$$
$$\_\_\_ \times \_\_\_ = \_\_\_$$
$$\_\_\_$$

Use the Expanded Notation Method to solve the problem. Complete the steps.

4. A farm stand sold 4 bushels of apples in one day. Each bushel of apples weighs 42 pounds. How many pounds of apples did the farm stand sell?

_____

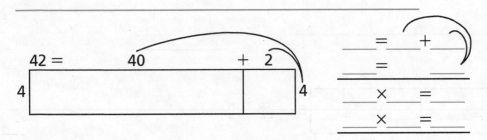

$$\_\_\_ = \_\_\_ + \_\_\_$$
$$\_\_\_ = \_\_\_$$
$$\_\_\_ \times \_\_\_ = \_\_\_$$
$$\_\_\_ \times \_\_\_ = \_\_\_$$

Draw an area model and use the Expanded Notation Method to solve the problem.

5. A marina needs to replace the boards on their pier. The pier is 7 feet by 39 feet. What is the area of the boards that need to be replaced?

_____

_____

▶ Use the Algebraic Notation Method to Multiply

Another numerical multiplication method that can be represented by an area model is the **Algebraic Notation Method**. This method also decomposes the two-digit factor into tens and ones and then uses the Distributive Property.

Use the Algebraic Notation Method to solve each problem. Complete the steps.

4. 8 · 62

62 = _____ _____ + _____

_____

$8 \cdot 62 = \_\_\_ \cdot (\_\_\_ + \_\_\_)$
$= 480 + 16$
$= 496$

5. 2 · 97

97 = _____ _____ + _____

_____

$2 \cdot 97 = \_\_\_ \cdot (\_\_\_ + \_\_\_)$
$= 180 + 14$
$= 194$

Draw an area model and use the Algebraic Notation Method to solve the problem.

6. There are 9 members on the school's golf team. Each golfer hit a bucket of 68 golf balls at the driving range. How many golf balls did the entire team hit?

_____

7. What is the first step in the Algebraic Notation Method?

_____

► Practice Different Methods

Fill in the blanks in the following solutions.

3. 4 × 86

Expanded Notation

$$86 = \underline{\qquad} + 6$$

$$\times\ 4 = \underline{\hspace{3cm}}$$
$$\underline{\qquad\qquad\qquad}$$

$$4 \times \underline{\qquad} = \underline{\qquad}$$

$$\underline{\qquad} \times 6 = 24$$
$$\underline{\qquad\qquad\qquad}$$

$$\underline{\qquad}$$

Algebraic Notation

$$4 \cdot 86 = \underline{\qquad} \cdot (80 + 6)$$

$$= 320 + \underline{\qquad}$$

$$= \underline{\qquad}$$

4. 4 × 68

Expanded Notation

$$\underline{\qquad} = 60 + 8$$

$$\times\ 4 = \underline{\hspace{3cm}}$$
$$\underline{\qquad\qquad\qquad}$$

$$4 \times \underline{\qquad} = \underline{\qquad}$$

$$\underline{\qquad} \times 8 = 32$$
$$\underline{\qquad\qquad\qquad}$$

$$\underline{\qquad}$$

Algebraic Notation

$$4 \cdot 68 = 4 \cdot (\underline{\qquad} + \underline{\qquad})$$

$$= 240 + \underline{\qquad}$$

$$= \underline{\qquad}$$

Solve using a numerical method. Draw the related area model.

5. 5 × 64 = _____

6. 6 × 72 = _____

7. 7 × 92 = _____

8. 8 × 53 = _____

9. 5 × 46 = _____

10. 6 × 27 = _____

1. Use the numbers on the tiles to complete the steps to find
   20 × 40 by factoring the tens.

2	4	6
8	10	20

600   800

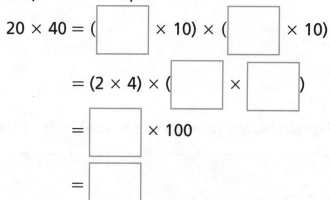

$20 × 40 = ($ ▢ $× 10) × ($ ▢ $× 10)$

$= (2 × 4) × ($ ▢ $×$ ▢ $)$

$=$ ▢ $× 100$

$=$ ▢

2. Select the expression that is equivalent to 36 × 25.
   Mark all that apply.

   Ⓐ 30 × 6 + 20 × 5

   Ⓑ (30 × 20) + (30 × 5) + (6 × 20) + (6 × 5)

   Ⓒ (5 × 6) + (5 × 3 tens) + (2 tens × 6) + (2 tens × 3 tens)

   Ⓓ 30 × (20 + 5) + 6 × (20 + 5)

   Ⓔ 30 + 15 + 12 + 6

3. There are 24 pencils in a box. If there are 90 boxes,
   how many pencils are there?

   _____ pencils

4. A clown bought 18 bags of round balloons with 20 balloons
   in each bag. He bought 26 bags of long balloons with
   35 balloons in each bag. How many more long balloons
   are there than round balloons? Show your work.

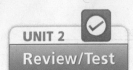
5. Draw an area model for 7 × 682.

Explain how you used the model to find the product.

6. For numbers 6a–6e, choose Yes or No to tell whether the equation is true.

6a. 8 × 4 = 32　　　　　　　　○ Yes　　○ No

6b. 8 × 400 = 32,000　　　　○ Yes　　○ No

6c. 80 × 40 = 3,200　　　　　○ Yes　　○ No

6d. 8 × 4,000 = 32,000　　　○ Yes　　○ No

6e. 800 × 40 = 320,000　　　○ Yes　　○ No

7. Find the product of 4 × 52.

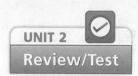
8. Use the numbers on the tiles to complete the area model for 29 × 48.

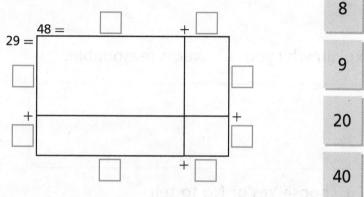

8

9

20

40

Show how to use the area model and expanded notation to find 29 × 48.

9. Estimate 15 × 34 by rounding each number to the nearest ten.

10. For numbers 10a–10d, choose True or False to describe the statement.

10a. 8 × 93 is greater than 8 × 90.　　　○ True　　○ False

10b. An estimate of 8 × 93 is 2,700.　　　○ True　　○ False

10c. 8 × 93 = (8 × 9) + (8 × 3)　　　　○ True　　○ False

10d. 8 × 93 is less than 800.　　　　　○ True　　○ False

11. Find 4 × 7,342.

Use estimation to explain why your answer is reasonable.

12. For numbers 12a–12d, choose Yes or No to tell whether the equation is true.

12a. 5 × 60 = 30   ○ Yes   ○ No

12b. 500 × 6 = 30,000   ○ Yes   ○ No

12c. 50 × 600 = 30,000   ○ Yes   ○ No

12d. 5 × 60,000 = 300,000 ○ Yes   ○ No

13. The best estimate for 78 × 50 is that it must be greater than ___?___ but less than ___?___.

Select one number from each column to make the sentence true.

Greater than	Less than
○ 3,200	○ 3,200
○ 3,500	○ 3,500
○ 4,000	○ 4,000
○ 4,200	○ 4,200

14. Choose the number from the box to complete the statement.

The product of 39 and 22 is closest to ⬚.

300
400
800
8,000

15. A bus tour of New York City costs $48 per person. A group of 7 people go on the tour. What is the cost for the group? Explain how you found your answer.

16. There is a book sale at the library. The price for each book is $4. If 239 books are sold, how much money will be made at the sale?

  Ⓐ $235

  Ⓑ $243

  Ⓒ $826

  Ⓓ $956

17. Volunteers are needed at the animal shelter. If 245 boys and 304 girls each volunteer to work 3 hours, how many volunteer hours is this?

Part A

Identify any extra information given in the problem.
Explain your reasoning.

Part B

Solve the problem. Show your work.

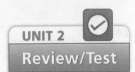

18. Select an expression that is equivalent to 7 × 800.
    Mark all that apply.

    Ⓐ 8 + (100 × 7) + 10   Ⓒ (7 × 80) × 10

    Ⓑ (8 × 7) × (100 × 1)   Ⓓ (8 + 7) × (100 + 1)

19. Joe makes belts. He has 9 buckles. He uses 12 rivets on
    each of 4 belts and 15 rivets on each of 2 belts. He has
    22 rivets left over. How many rivets are on the belts?

    Part A
    Identify any extra information given in the problem.

    ┌───┐
    │   │
    │   │
    └───┘

    Part B
    Solve the problem. Show your work.

    ┌───┐
    │   │
    │   │
    └───┘

20. Draw an area model for 7 × 5,432. Then write an
    equation to match your model.

    Equation: _____ × _____ = _____

21. Use the numbers on the tiles to complete
    the steps to find the solution to 4 × 65.

    4 × 65 = _____ × (60 + _____)

    　　　　= (4 × _____) + (4 × _____)

    　　　　= _____ + 20

    　　　　= _____

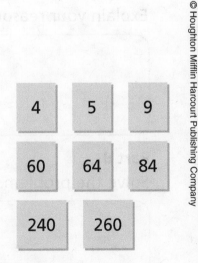

4	5	9
60	64	84
240	260	

Family Letter

Content Overview

Dear Family,

Your child is familiar with multiplication from earlier units. Unit 3 of *Math Expressions* extends the concepts used in multiplication to teach your child division. The main goals of this unit are to:

• Learn methods for dividing whole numbers up to four digits.

• Use estimates to check the reasonableness of answers.

• Solve problems involving division and remainders.

Your child will learn and practice techniques such as the Place Value Sections, Expanded Notation, and Digit-by-Digit methods to gain speed and accuracy in division. At first, your child will learn to use patterns and multiplication to divide. Later, your child will learn to use the methods with divisors from 2 to 9. Then your child will learn to divide when there is a zero in the quotient or dividend and to watch out for potential problems involving these situations.

Examples of Division Methods:

Your child may use whatever method he or she chooses as long as he or she can explain it. Some children like to use different methods.

Place Value Sections Method	Expanded Notation Method	Digit-by-Digit Method

Place Value Sections Method:

$$60 + 6 = 66$$

5	330	30
	− 300	30
	30	0

Expanded Notation Method:

$$\begin{array}{r} 6 \\ 60 \end{array}\Big] 66$$

$$5\overline{)330}$$
$$-300$$
$$\overline{30}$$
$$-30$$
$$\overline{0}$$

Digit-by-Digit Method:

$$\begin{array}{r} 66 \\ 5\overline{)330} \\ -30 \\ \hline 30 \\ -30 \\ \hline 0 \end{array}$$

Your child will also learn to interpret remainders in the context of the problem being solved; for example, when the remainder alone is the answer to a word problem.

Finally, your child will apply this knowledge to solve mixed problems with one or more steps and using all four operations.

If you have questions or problems, please contact me.

Sincerely,
Your child's teacher

© Houghton Mifflin Harcourt Publishing Company

CA CC

Unit 3 addresses the following standard from the *Common Core State Standards for Mathematics with California Additions*: **4.NBT.6** and all Mathematical Practices.

Un vistazo general al contenido

Estimada familia:

En unidades anteriores su niño se ha familiarizado con la multiplicación. La Unidad 3 de *Math Expressions* amplía los conceptos usados en la multiplicación para que su niño aprenda la división. Los objetivos principales de esta unidad son:

• aprender métodos para dividir números enteros de hasta cuatro dígitos.

• usar la estimación para comprobar si las respuestas son razonables.

• resolver problemas que requieran división y residuos.

Su niño aprenderá y practicará técnicas tales como las de Secciones de valor posicional, Notación extendida y Dígito por dígito, para adquirir rapidez y precisión en la división. Al principio, su niño aprenderá a usar patrones y la multiplicación para dividir. Más adelante, usará los métodos con divisores de 2 a 9. Luego, aprenderá a dividir cuando haya un cero en el cociente o en el dividendo, y a detectar problemas que pueden surgir en esas situaciones.

Ejemplos de métodos de división:

Secciones de valor posicional	Notación extendida	Dígito por dígito

$$60 + 6 = 66$$

$$
\begin{array}{c|c|c}
5 & 330 & 30 \\
 & -300 & 30 \\
\hline
 & 30 & 0
\end{array}
$$

$$
\begin{array}{r}
6 \\
60 \enclose{longdiv}{66} \\
5\,\overline{)330} \\
-300 \\
\hline
30 \\
-30 \\
\hline
0
\end{array}
$$

$$
\begin{array}{r}
66 \\
5\overline{)330} \\
-30 \\
\hline
30 \\
-30 \\
\hline
0
\end{array}
$$

Su niño puede usar el método que elija siempre y cuando pueda explicarlo. A algunos niños les gusta usar métodos diferentes.

Su niño también aprenderá a interpretar los residuos en el contexto del problema que se esté resolviendo; por ejemplo, cuando solamente el residuo es la respuesta a un problema.

Por último, su niño aplicará este conocimiento para resolver problemas mixtos de uno o más pasos, usando las cuatro operaciones.

Si tiene alguna pregunta o comentario, por favor comuníquese conmigo.

Atentamente,
El maestro de su niño

© Houghton Mifflin Harcourt Publishing Company

 CA CC

En la Unidad 3 se aplican los siguientes estándares auxiliares, contenidos en los *Estándares estatales comunes de matemáticas con adiciones para California*: **4.NBT.6** y todos los de prácticas matemáticas.

Name _____ Date _____

▶ Divide with Remainders

The remainder must be less than the divisor.
If it is not, increase the quotient.

$$
\begin{array}{r} 3 \\ 5\overline{)23} \\ -15 \\ \hline 8 \text{ no} \\ 8 > 5 \end{array}
\longrightarrow
\begin{array}{r} 4 \text{ R3} \\ 5\overline{)23} \\ -20 \\ \hline 3 \text{ yes} \\ 3 < 5 \end{array}
\qquad
\begin{array}{r} 8 \\ 9\overline{)87} \\ -72 \\ \hline 15 \text{ no} \\ 15 > 9 \end{array}
\longrightarrow
\begin{array}{r} 9 \text{ R6} \\ 9\overline{)87} \\ -81 \\ \hline 6 \text{ yes} \\ 6 < 9 \end{array}
$$

Divide with remainders.

1. $2\overline{)19}$

2. $7\overline{)50}$

3. $9\overline{)48}$

4. $5\overline{)48}$

5. $6\overline{)19}$

6. $3\overline{)25}$

Divide. Multiply to check the last problem in each row.

7. $6\overline{)27}$

8. $4\overline{)30}$

9. $\begin{array}{r} 5 \text{ R4} \\ 7\overline{)39} \\ -35 \\ \hline 4 \end{array}$ $\qquad$ $7 \cdot 5 + 4 =$
$35 + 4 = 39$

10. $8\overline{)43}$

11. $5\overline{)26}$

12. $9\overline{)41}$

13. $5\overline{)32}$

14. $4\overline{)21}$

15. $3\overline{)22}$

▶ Multiplying and Dividing

Complete the steps.

1. Sam divides 738 by 6. He uses the Place Value
   Sections Method and the Expanded Notation Method.

   a. Sam thinks: I'll draw the Place Value Sections that I know from
   multiplication. To divide, I need to find how many hundreds,
   tens, and ones to find the unknown factor.

Place Value Sections Method	**Expanded Notation Method**

   __hundreds + __tens + __ones
   __00   __0   __

6	738		

   $6\overline{)738}$

   b. 6 × 100 = 600 will fit. 6 × 200 = 1,200 is too big.

   __00   +   _0   +   _

6	738		

   $6\overline{)738}$

   c. I have 138 left for the other sections.
   6 × 20 = 120 will fit. 6 × 30 = 180 is too big.

   100   +   _0   +   _

6	738 −600 138	138	

   $$\begin{array}{r} 100 \\ 6\overline{)738} \\ -\ 600 \\ \hline 138 \end{array}$$

   d. 6 × 3 = 18

   100   +   20   +   _   =   _____

6	738 −600 138	138 −120 18	18 0

   $$\begin{array}{r} 20 \\ 100 \\ 6\overline{)738} \\ -\ 600 \\ \hline 138 \\ -\ 120 \\ \hline 18 \end{array}$$

Relate 3-Digit Multiplication to Division

▶ Practice the Place Value Sections Method

Solve. Use Place Value Sections Method for division.

The sidewalk crew knows that the new sidewalk at the mall will be 3,915 square feet. It will be 9 feet wide. How long will it be? _____

$$\underline{400} + \underline{30} + \underline{5} = 435$$

	400	30	5
9 ft	3,915 −3,600	315 −270	45 −45
	315	45	0

2. The sidewalk at the theater will be 2,748 square feet. It will be 6 feet wide. How long will it be?

_____

$$\underline{\quad}00 + \underline{\quad}0 + \underline{\quad} = \underline{\quad}$$

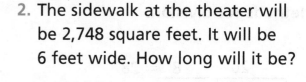

3. Pens are packaged in boxes of 8. The store is charged for a total of 4,576 pens. How many boxes of pens did they receive?_____

$$\underline{\quad}00 + \underline{\quad}0 + \underline{\quad} = \underline{\quad}$$

4. A factory has 2,160 erasers. They package them in groups of 5. How many packages of erasers does the factory have? _____

$$\underline{\quad} + \underline{\quad} + \underline{\quad} = \underline{\quad}$$

5. A party planner has 834 small flowers to make party favors. She will put 3 flowers in each party favor. How many party favors can she make? _____

$$\underline{\quad} + \underline{\quad} + \underline{\quad} = \underline{\quad}$$

6. An artist has 956 tiles to use in a design. He plans to arrange the tiles in group of 4 tiles. How many groups of 4 tiles can he make?

_____

$$\underline{\quad} + \underline{\quad} + \underline{\quad} = \underline{\quad}$$

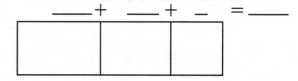

CA CC Content Standards **4.NBT.6**
Mathematical Practices **MP.2, MP.7, MP.8**

Name _____ **Date** _____

▶ 2-Digit and 4-Digit Quotients

Solve. Use the Place Value Sections and the Expanded Notation Methods for division.

1.

```
        20   +    8   = 28
     ┌────────┬────────┐
   9 │  252   │   72   │
     │ − 180  │ − 72   │
     └────────┴────────┘
        72         0
```

9)252‾

2.

```
         _0   +        =  __
     ┌────────┬────────┐
   6 │  162   │        │
     │        │        │
     └────────┴────────┘
```

6)162‾

3.

```
      __,000  +   __00  +    _0  +    _  =  ____
     ┌────────┬────────┬────────┬────────┐
   8 │ 8,984  │        │        │        │
     │        │        │        │        │
     └────────┴────────┴────────┴────────┘
```

8)8,984‾

4.

```
      __,000  +   __00  +    _0  +    _  =  ____
     ┌────────┬────────┬────────┬────────┐
   3 │ 7,722  │        │        │        │
     │        │        │        │        │
     └────────┴────────┴────────┴────────┘
```

3)7,722‾

▶ **Practice**

Divide.

6. 4)868   7. 6)5,142   8. 3)4,395

9. 4)332   10. 7)1,617   11. 7)939

12. 2)4,276   13. 6)2,576   14. 7)441

15. 9)3,735   16. 7)406   17. 3)9,954

▶ Practice

Divide.

6. $5\overline{)965}$

7. $8\overline{)128}$

8. $8\overline{)928}$

9. $3\overline{)716}$

10. $4\overline{)4,596}$

11. $4\overline{)982}$

12. $3\overline{)6,342}$

13. $8\overline{)578}$

14. $5\overline{)1,155}$

15. $6\overline{)3,336}$

16. $7\overline{)672}$

17. $3\overline{)4,152}$

Digit-by-Digit Method

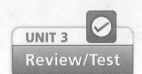
Name _____ **Date** _____

1. For 1a–1d, choose True or False to indicate if the statement is correct.

   1a. $245 \div 6 = 40 \text{ R}5$ ⚬ True ⚬ False

   1b. $803 \div 2 = 400$ ⚬ True ⚬ False

   1c. $492 \div 7 = 69 \text{ R}7$ ⚬ True ⚬ False

   1d. $355 \div 5 = 71$ ⚬ True ⚬ False

2. A train has a total of 216 seats in 3 cars. Each train car has the same number of seats. How many seats are in each train car?

   _____ seats

3. Kayla puts together gift boxes of fruit to sell at her fruit stand. She places exactly 6 pieces of fruit in each box. She only sells full boxes of fruit.

   Part A

   Kayla has 256 apples. How many boxes of fruit can she fill? Explain how you found your answer.

   Part B

   Kayla has enough peaches to fill 31 gift boxes. How many apples and peaches did Kayla put in gift boxes to sell at her fruit stand? Show your work.

4. Margaret is dividing 829 by 4.

Part A

Explain why Margaret needs to write a zero in the tens place of the quotient.

Part B

How would the digit in the tens place of the quotient change if Margaret were dividing 829 by 2?

5. A storage shelf where Carmen works can hold about 165 pounds. The storage shelf can hold 8 boxes of car parts. About how many pounds does each box weigh? Does this problem require an exact answer or an estimate? Then find the answer.

6. What is 945 ÷ 5?

(A) 189   (C) 199

(B) 190   (D) 209

7. Divide 4,124 by 2.

8. Joshua carried 52 loads of sand to make a play area. Each load weighed 21 pounds. How many pounds of sand does Joshua use to make the play area? Use the numbers and symbols on the keypad to write the expression needed to solve this problem. Then solve the problem.

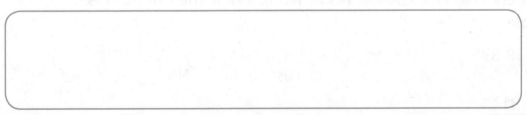

7	8	9
4	5	6
1	2	3
0	÷	×

expression: _____

_____ pounds

9. There are 118 boys and 121 girls signed up for a volleyball league. The coaches first make teams of 9 players and then assign any remaining players to make some of the teams have 10 players.

Part A

How many teams of 10 players will there be? Explain.

Part B

How many teams of 9 players will there be? Explain.

10. A florist has 2,388 flowers to make into small bouquets. She wants 6 flowers in each bouquet. How many bouquets can she make? Complete the Place Value Sections to solve.

____00   +   ____0   +   ____ = _____ bouquets

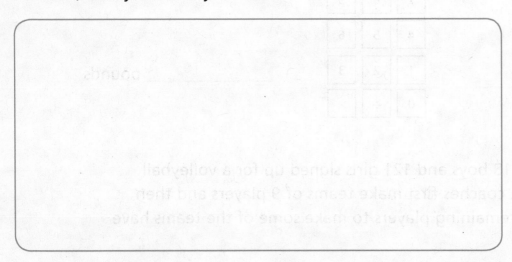

11. Divide 7,433 by 7. Show your work.

12. For numbers 12a–12d, choose Yes or No to tell if the quotient is reasonable.

12a.
$$\begin{array}{r} 39\text{ R}3 \\ 6\overline{)297} \end{array}$$
○ Yes   ○ No

12b.
$$\begin{array}{r} 814 \\ 4\overline{)3,256} \end{array}$$
○ Yes   ○ No

12c.
$$\begin{array}{r} 228\text{ R}5 \\ 8\overline{)4,229} \end{array}$$
○ Yes   ○ No

12d.
$$\begin{array}{r} 1,007\text{ R}1 \\ 8\overline{)5,136} \end{array}$$
○ Yes   ○ No

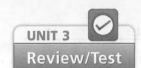
13. Hailey finds 24 seashells on Friday and another 38 seashells on Saturday. She shares as many of the seashells as she can equally among herself and 3 friends. She keeps the leftover seashells for herself. How many seashells does Hailey get? Show your work.

14. Ethan has 203 geodes to put into display cases. Each case holds 8 geodes. How many cases does Ethan need to hold all the geodes? Explain how you know.

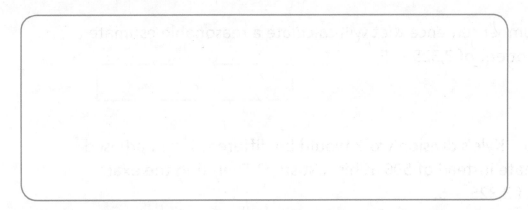

15. Select one number from each column to make the equation true.

$$5{,}155 \div 3 = \boxed{} \ R \ \boxed{}$$

Quotient	Remainder
○ 1,715	○ 1
○ 1,717	○ 2
○ 1,718	○ 3
○ 1,720	○ 4

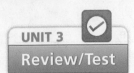

16. Julie divided 2,526 by 6 and found a quotient of 421.
For 16a–16c, choose True or False to tell if the
statement is correct.

16a. 2,400 ÷ 6 = 400, so 421 makes sense. ○ True ○ False

16b. 2,526 ÷ 6 = 421 R5 ○ True ○ False

16c. 421 × 6 = 2,526, so 421 makes sense. ○ True ○ False

17. Which expression has a quotient of 400? Circle all that apply.

| 1,600 ÷ 4 | 2,000 ÷ 5 | 400 ÷ 4 | 3,600 ÷ 9 |

18. Kyle wrote his first step in dividing 3,325 ÷ 5 using the Expanded
Notation Method.

$$
\begin{array}{r}
500 \\
5\overline{)3{,}325} \\
-2{,}500 \\
\hline
825
\end{array}
$$

Part A

Write a number sentence that will calculate a reasonable estimate
for the quotient of 3,325 ÷ 5.

Part B

Explain how Kyle's division work would be different if he had used
your estimate instead of 500 as his first step? Then find the exact
quotient of 3,325 ÷ 5.

Family Letter

Content Overview

Dear Family,

In Unit 4 of Math Expressions, your child will apply the skills he or she has learned about operations with whole numbers while solving real world problems involving addition, subtraction, multiplication, and division.

Your child will simplify and evaluate expressions. Parentheses will be introduced to show which operation should be done first. The symbols "=" and "≠" will be used to show whether numbers and expressions are equal.

Other topics of study in this unit include situation and solution equations for addition and subtraction, as well as multiplication and division. Your child will use situation equations to represent real world problems and solution equations to solve the problems. This method of representing a problem is particularly helpful when the problems contain greater numbers and students cannot solve mentally.

Your child will also solve multiplication and addition comparison problems and compare these types of problems identifying what is the same or different.

Addition Comparison	Multiplication Comparison
Angela is 14 years old. She is 4 years older than Damarcus. How old is Damarcus?	Shawn colored 5 pages in a coloring book. Anja colored 4 times as many pages as Shawn colored. How many pages did Anja color?

Students learn that in the addition problem they are adding 4, while in the multiplication problem, they are multiplying by 4.

Your child will apply this knowledge to solve word problems using all four operations and involving one or more steps.

Finally, your child will find factor pairs for whole numbers and generate and analyze numerical and geometric patterns.

If you have any questions or comments, please call or write to me.

Sincerely,
Your child's teacher

CA CC

Unit 4 addresses the following standards from the *Common Core State Standards for Mathematics with California Additions*: **4.OA.1, 4.OA.2, 4.OA.3, 4.OA.4, 4.OA.5, 4.NBT.4, 4.NBT.5, 4.NBT.6, 4.MD.2**, and all Mathematical Practices.

Properties and Algebraic Notation **47**

Estimada familia:

En la Unidad 4 de Math Expressions, su hijo aplicará las destrezas relacionadas con operaciones de números enteros que ha adquirido, resolviendo problemas cotidianos que involucran suma, resta, multiplicación y división.

Su hijo simplificará y evaluará expresiones. Se introducirán los paréntesis como una forma de mostrar cuál operación deberá completarse primero. Los signos "=" y "≠" se usarán para mostrar si los números o las expresiones son iguales o no.

Otros temas de estudio en esta unidad incluyen ecuaciones de situación y de solución para la suma y resta, así como para la multiplicación y división. Su hijo usará ecuaciones de situación para representar problemas de la vida cotidiana y ecuaciones de solución para resolver esos problemas. Este método para representar problemas es particularmente útil cuando los problemas involucran números grandes y los estudiantes no pueden resolverlos mentalmente.

Su hijo también resolverá problemas de comparación de multiplicación y suma, y comparará este tipo de problemas para identificar las semejanzas y diferencias.

Comparación de suma	Comparación de multiplicación
Ángela tiene 14 años. Ella es 4 años mayor que Damarcus. ¿Cuántos años tiene Damarcus?	Shawn coloreó 5 páginas de un libro. Ana coloreó 4 veces ese número de páginas. ¿Cuántas páginas coloreó Ana?

Los estudiantes aprenderán que en el problema de suma están sumando 4, mientras que en el problema de multiplicación, están multiplicando por 4.

Su hijo aplicará estos conocimientos para resolver problemas de uno o más pasos usando las cuatro operaciones.

Finalmente, su hijo hallará pares de factores para números enteros y generará y analizará patrones numéricos y geométricos.

Si tiene alguna pregunta por favor comuníquese conmigo.

Atentamente,
El maestro de su niño

CA CC

En la Unidad 4 se aplican los siguientes estándares auxiliares, contenidos en los *Estándares estatales comunes de matemáticas con adiciones para California*: **4.OA.1, 4.OA.2, 4.OA.3, 4.OA.4, 4.OA.5, 4.NBT.4, 4.NBT.5, 4.NBT.6, 4.MD.2** y todos los de prácticas matemáticas.

▶ Discuss Inverse Operations

When you add, you put two groups together. When you subtract, you find an unknown addend or take away one group from another. Addition and subtraction are inverse operations. They undo each other.

Addends are numbers that are added to make a sum. You can find two addends for a sum by breaking apart the number.

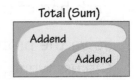

A break-apart drawing can help you find all eight related addition and subtraction equations for two addends.

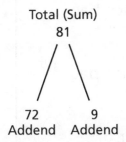

Total (Sum)
81
72 9
Addend Addend

$81 = 72 + 9$ $72 + 9 = 81$

$81 = 9 + 72$ $9 + 72 = 81$

$72 = 81 - 9$ $81 - 9 = 72$

$9 = 81 - 72$ $81 - 72 = 9$

9. Which equations show the Commutative Property?

_____

10. What is the total in each equation? Where is the total in a subtraction equation?

_____

Solve each equation.

11. $50 = 30 + p$

$p =$ _____

12. $q + 20 = 60$

$q =$ _____

13. $90 - v = 50$

$v =$ _____

14. Write the eight related addition and subtraction equations for the break-apart drawing.

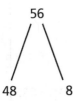

56
48   8

_____   _____

_____   _____

_____   _____

_____   _____

Name _____ **Date** _____

CA CC Content Standards **4.OA.3**
Mathematical Practices **MP.1, MP.3, MP.4, MP.6**

▶ Discuss the Steps

1. Mr. Stills makes bags of school supplies for the 9 students in his class. He has 108 pencils and 72 erasers. He puts the same number of pencils and the same number of erasers into each bag. How many more pencils than erasers are in each bag of school supplies?

   Solve the problem by finishing Nicole's and David's methods. Discuss what is alike and what is different about the methods.

Nicole's Method

Write an equation for each step.

Divide to find the number of pencils that Mr. Stills puts in each bag of school supplies.

$108 \div 9 =$ _____

Divide to find the number of erasers that Mr. Stills puts in each bag of school supplies.

$72 \div 9 =$ _____

Subtract the number of erasers in each bag from the number of pencils in each bag.

$12 - 8 =$ _____

There are _____ more pencils than erasers in each bag of school supplies.

David's Method

Write an equation for the whole problem.

Let $p =$ how many more pencils than erasers are in each bag of school supplies

The number of pencils in each bag of school supplies.

The number of erasers in each bag of school supplies.

_____ $\div$ 9 $-$ _____ $\div$ 9 $= p$

$12 - 8 = p$

_____ $= p$

There are _____ more pencils than erasers in each bag of school supplies.

Solve Multistep Problems

▶ Discuss the Steps (continued)

2. John is selling bags of popcorn for a school fundraiser. So far, John has sold 45 bags of popcorn for $5 each. His goal is to earn $300 for the school fundraiser. How many more bags of popcorn must John sell to reach his goal?

Solve the problem by writing an equation for each step. Then solve the problem by writing one equation for the whole problem.

Write an equation for each step.

Multiply to find how much money John has earned so far selling popcorn.

_____ × $5 = _____

Subtract to find how much money John has left to earn to reach his goal.

$300 − _____

Divide to find the number of bags of popcorn John must sell to reach his goal.

$75 ÷ $5 = _____

John must sell _____ more bags of popcorn to reach his goal.

Write an equation for the whole problem.

Let b = the number of bags of popcorn John must sell to reach his goal.

John's fundraiser goal amount.　　Amount of money John has raised so far.

(_____ − _____ × $5) ÷ $5 = b

($300 − $_____) ÷ $5 = b

$_____ ÷ $5 = b

_____ = b

John must sell _____ more bags of popcorn to reach his goal.

▶ Find Factor Pairs

> A factor pair for a number is two whole numbers whose product is that number. For example, 2 and 5 is a factor pair for 10.

1. Draw arrays to show all the factor pairs for 12 on the grid below. The array for 1 and 12 is shown.

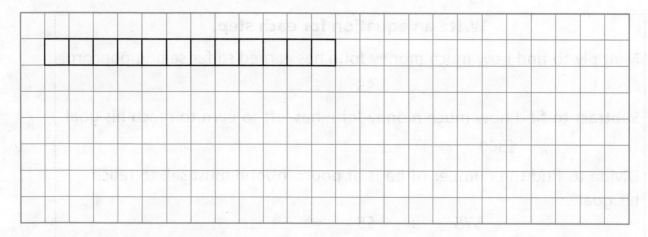

2. List all the factor pairs for 12. _____

Use the table to find all the factors pairs for each number.

3. 32

1	32
2	

4. 44

1	44

5. 100

1	100

List all the factor pairs for each number.

6. 29

7. 63

Factors and Prime Numbers

1. The number of ash trees on a tree farm is 5 times the number of pine trees. Choose one expression from each column to create an equation that compares the number of ash trees (a) and pine trees (p).

○ a − 5	○ p
○ 5a	○ 5p
○ a	○ p + 5
○ a ÷ 5	○ p − 5

= (between the two columns)

2. Katie canned 182 quarts of tomatoes last week. She canned 259 quarts of tomatoes this week. How many quarts of tomatoes (q) did Katie can over these two weeks? Write an equation. Then solve.

Equation: _____

$q = $ _____ quarts

3. Eliot sends 217 text messages each week. Write equations to find how many text messages he sends in 4 weeks and in 7 weeks.

Equations: _____

_____

Use the equations to complete the table.

Weeks	Total Text Messages
1	217
4	
7	

4. Solve for n.

$(16 + 12) \div (11 − 7) = n$ $n = \boxed{}$

5. There are 1,342 players in the baseball league. That is 2 times the number of players in the football league. How many players are in the football league? Write an equation. Then solve.

6. A school ordered 688 T-shirts in 3 sizes: small, medium, and large. There are 296 small and 268 medium T-shirts. How many large T-shirts were ordered? Select numbers from the list to complete the equation. Then solve.

| 3 | 268 | 296 | 688 |

$$l = \boxed{} - \left(\boxed{} + \boxed{} \right)$$

$l = $ _____ large T-shirts

7. Select the factor pair for 45. Mark all that apply.

Ⓐ 4, 11   Ⓒ 6, 7   Ⓔ 1, 45

Ⓑ 3, 15   Ⓓ 4, 12   Ⓕ 5, 9

8. Is a multiple of the prime number 3 also a prime number? Circle your answer.

Yes   No

Explain your reasoning.

9. For numbers 9a–9e, choose Yes or No to tell whether the number is prime.

9a. 49   ○ Yes   ○ No

9b. 53   ○ Yes   ○ No

9c. 63   ○ Yes   ○ No

9d. 37   ○ Yes   ○ No

9e. 51   ○ Yes   ○ No

10. Classify each number from the list as being a multiple of 2, 3, or 5. Write each number in the correct box. A number can be written in more than one box.

| 18   30   20   24   55   39 |

Multiple of 2	**Multiple of 3**	**Multiple of 5**

11. Use the rule to find the next 3 terms in the pattern.

Rule: multiply by 2

4, 8, 16, 32, ☐ , ☐ , ☐ , …

12. Draw the next term of the pattern.

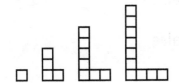

13. A team of workers is building a 942-foot trail. They plan to complete 6 feet per hour. How many hours will it take to build the trail?

Choose the equation that can be used to solve this problem. Mark all that apply.

Ⓐ $942 \times 6 = h$ Ⓓ $6 \times h = 942$

Ⓑ $942 \div 6 = h$ Ⓔ $6 = 942 \times h$

Ⓒ $942 \div h = 6$ Ⓕ $942 = 6 \div h$

14. Roger first ships a large number of packages. Then he ships 3,820 more packages. Roger ships 22,540 packages in all. How many packages did he ship first? Identify the type of comparison as addition or multiplication. Then write and solve an equation to solve the problem.

Type of comparison: _____

Equation: _____

Answer: _____ packages

15. For numbers 15a–15d, select True or False for the calculation.

15a. $72 \div (6 + 2) = 9$ ○ True   ○ False

15b. $(2 + 7) + (6 - 2) = 36$ ○ True   ○ False

15c. $(12 + 8) \div 4 = 10 \div (5 - 3)$ ○ True   ○ False

15d. $(35 - 8) \div (2 + 1) = 32$ ○ True   ○ False

16. Charlotte made this pictograph to show the number of dogs attending a dog training class this week.

Dogs in Training Class

Monday	🐾 🐾 🐾
Wednesday	🐾 🐾
Friday	🐾 🐾 🐾 🐾 🐾 🐾
Saturday	🐾 🐾 🐾 🐾 🐾 🐾 🐾 🐾

🐾 = 3 dogs

Part A

How many fewer dogs were in training class on Monday than on Friday? Write and solve an equation.

Equation: _____

Answer: _____ fewer dogs

Part B

Choose the number that makes the sentence true.

Charlotte forgot to include Thursday on her graph. There were two times as many dogs at Thursday's class than at Monday's class.

There were
| 2 |
| 6 |
| 15 |
| 18 |
dogs in the training class on Thursday.

Part C

Explain how you determined the number of dogs at Thursday's class.

_____

17. The Ruiz family bought 2 adult tickets and 4 child tickets to the fair. The adult tickets cost $8 each. The child tickets cost $3 each.

Part A

Complete the equation Zach and Alannah wrote to find the total cost of the tickets bought by the Ruiz family.

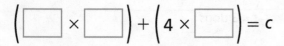

$$\left(\boxed{} \times \boxed{} \right) + \left(4 \times \boxed{} \right) = c$$

Part B

Zach's answer is $72, and Alannah's answer is $28. Who has the wrong answer? Explain what error he or she made.

18. A store has 4 bins of planet posters with 23 posters in each bin. It has 3 bins of planet calendars with 26 calendars in each bin. Yesterday, 72 calendars were sold. How many planet posters and calendars are left in all? Explain how you found your answer, and how you know if your answer is reasonable.

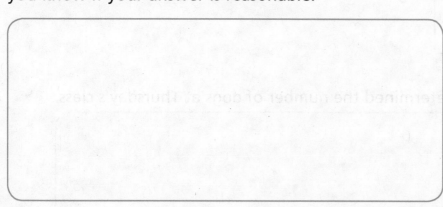

Family Letter

Content Overview

Dear Family,

This unit is about the metric measurement system. During this unit, students will become familiar with metric units of length, capacity, mass, and time, as well as the size of each when compared to each other.

One **meter** is about the distance an adult man can reach, or a little longer than a yard.

One **liter** is about two large glasses of liquid, or a little more than a quart.

One **gram** is about the mass of a paper clip or a single peanut. One **kilogram** is a little more than 2 pounds.

Students will also discover that the metric system is based on multiples of 10. Prefixes in the names of metric measurements tell the size of a measure compared to the size of the base unit.

Units of Length

kilometer	hectometer	decameter	meter	decimeter	centimeter	millimeter
km	hm	dam	m	dm	cm	mm
10 × 10 × 10 × larger	10 × 10 × larger	10 × larger	1 m	10 × smaller	10 × 10 × smaller	10 × 10 × 10 × smaller
1 km = 1,000 m	1 hm = 100 m	1 dam = 10 m		10 dm = 1 m	100 cm = 1 m	1,000 mm = 1 m

The most commonly used length units are the **kilometer, meter, centimeter,** and **millimeter.**

The most commonly used capacity units are the **liter** and **milliliter.**

The most commonly used units of mass are the **gram, kilogram,** and **milligram.**

If you have any questions or comments, please call or write to me.

Sincerely,
Your child's teacher

CA CC

Unit 5 addresses the following standards from the *Common Core State Standards for Mathematics with California Additions:* **4.MD.1, 4.MD.2, 4.MD.3, 4.MD.4** and all Mathematical Practices.

Carta a la familia

Un vistazo general al contenido

Estimada familia:

Esta unidad trata del sistema métrico de medidas. Durante esta unidad, los estudiantes se familiarizarán con unidades métricas de longitud, capacidad y masa, así como con el tamaño de cada una comparada con las otras.

Un **metro** es aproximadamente la distancia que un hombre adulto puede alcanzar extendiendo el brazo, o un poco más de una yarda.

Un **litro** es aproximadamente dos vasos grandes de líquido, o un poco más de un cuarto de galón.

Un **gramo** es aproximadamente la masa de un clip o un cacahuate. Un **kilogramo** es un poco más de 2 libras.

Los estudiantes también descubrirán que el sistema métrico está basado en múltiplos de 10. Los prefijos de los nombres de las medidas métricas indican el tamaño de la medida comparado con el tamaño de la unidad base.

Unidades de longitud						
kilómetro	hectómetro	decámetro	metro	decímetro	centímetro	milímetro
km	hm	dam	m	dm	cm	mm
10 × 10 × 10 × más grande	10 × 10 × más grande	10 × más grande	1 m	10 × más pequeño	10 × 10 × más pequeño	10 × 10 × 10 × más pequeño
1 km = 1,000 m	1 hm = 100 m	1 dam = 10 m		10 dm = 1 m	100 cm = 1 m	1,000 mm = 1 m

Las unidades de longitud más comunes son **kilómetro**, **metro**, **centímetro** y **milímetro**.

Las unidades de capacidad más comunes son **litro** y **mililitro**.

Las unidades de masa más comunes son **gramo**, **kilogramo** y **miligramo**.

Si tiene alguna pregunta o algún comentario, por favor comuníquese conmigo.

Atentamente,
El maestro de su niño

CA CC

En la Unidad 5 se aplican los siguientes estándares auxiliares, contenidos en los *Estándares estatales comunes de matemáticas con adiciones para California*: **4.MD.1, 4.MD.2, 4.MD.3, 4.MD.4** y todos los de prácticas matemáticas.

Measure Length

▶ Convert Metric Units of Measure

You can use a table to convert measurements.

20. How many decimeters are in one meter? _____

21. Complete the equation.
1 meter = _____ decimeters

22. Complete the table. Explain how you found the number of decimeters in 8 meters.

_____

_____

Meters	Decimeters
2	2 × 10 = 20
4	___ × 10 = ___
6	6 × ___ = ___
8	_____ = ___

You can also use a number line to convert measurements.

23. Complete the equation. 1 kilometer = _____ meters

24. Label the double number line to show how kilometers (km) and meters (m) are related.

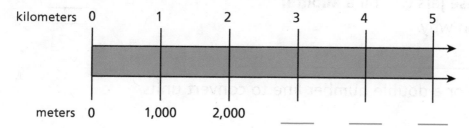

Solve each problem. Label your answers with the correct units.

25. Marsha drove her car 6,835 kilometers last year. How many meters did Marsha drive last year?

_____

26. John's television is 160 cm wide. How many millimeters wide is the television?

_____

Solve.

27. 5 m = _____ cm   28. 3 hm = _____ m   29. 7 km = _____ m

Name _____   **Date** _____

CA CC Content Standards **4.MD.1, 4.MD.2**
Mathematical Practices **MP.1, MP.2, MP.3, MP.6, MP.7**

> **VOCABULARY**
> liquid volume
> liter
> milliliter
> kiloliter

▶ Measure Liquid Volume

The base metric unit of **liquid volume** is a **liter**.

Units of Liquid Volume

kiloliter	hectoliter	decaliter	liter	deciliter	centiliter	milliliter
kL	hL	daL	L	dL	cL	mL
10 × 10 × 10 × larger	10 × 10 × larger	10 × larger	1 L	10 × smaller	10 × 10 × smaller	10 × 10 × 10 × smaller
1 kL = 1,000 L	1 hL = 100 L	1 daL = 10 L		10 dL = 1 L	100 cL = 1 L	1,000 mL = 1 L

Ms. Lee's class cut a two-liter plastic bottle in half to make a one-liter jar. They marked the outside to show equal parts.

1. How many **milliliters** of water will fit in the jar?

_____

2. How many of these jars will fill a **kiloliter** container? Explain why.

_____

You can use a table or a double number line to convert units of liquid measure.

3. Complete the table.

Liters	Deciliters	
3	3 × 10	= 30
5	___ × 10	= ___
7	7 × ___	= ___
12	___	= ___

4. Label the double number line to show how liters (L) and milliliters (mL) are related.

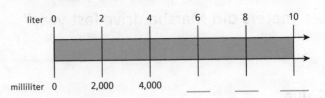

▶ Measure Mass

The basic unit of **mass** is the **gram**.

Units of Mass

kilogram	hectogram	decagram	gram	decigram	centigram	milligram
kg	hg	dag	g	dg	cg	mg
10 × 10 × 10 × larger	10 × 10 × larger	10 × larger	1 g	10 × smaller	10 × 10 × smaller	10 × 10 × 10 × smaller
1 kg = 1,000 g	1 hg = 100 g	1 dag = 10 g		10 dg = 1 g	100 cg = 1 g	1,000 mg = 1 g

8. How many **milligrams** are equal to 1 gram?

_____

9. How many grams are equal to 1 kilogram?

_____

If you weighed 1 mL of water, you would find that its mass would be one gram (1 g).

10. Is the gram a small or large unit of measurement? Explain your thinking.

_____

You can use a table or a double number line to convert units of mass.

11. Complete the table.

Grams	Centigrams
4	4 × 100 = 400
8	___ × 100 = ___
12	12 × ___ = ___
15	___ = ___

12. Label the double number line to show how kilograms (kg) and grams (g) are related.

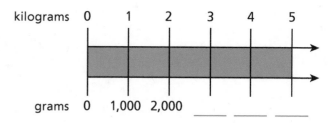

▶ Practice Converting Metric Units

Solve.

13. Martin measured the mass in grams of four different objects and recorded the information in the table below. Complete the table to find the mass of each object in milligrams.

Grams	Milligrams
4	4,000
7	
11	
15	

14. Olivia bought four different-sized containers and filled them each with water. She recorded the liquid volume of each container in liters below. Complete the table to find the liquid volume of each container in centiliters.

Liters	Centiliters
1	
3	
4	400
6	

15. Hayden has a crayon with a mass of 8 grams. Complete the double number line to find the mass of the crayon in centigrams.

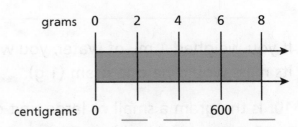

16. Jennifer buys a 2-liter bottle of apple juice and a 3-liter bottle of orange juice at the market. How many deciliters of juice does Jennifer buy in all?

_____

17. Elena has a cat with a mass of 4 kilograms. Ginger's cat has a mass that is 2 times as much as Elena's cat. What is the mass of Ginger's cat in grams?

_____

VOCABULARY
line plot

▶ Make a Line Plot

A **line plot** displays data above a number line. Jamal asked his classmates about the time they spend reading. He organized the answers in the table.

Time Spent Reading	Number of Students
0 hour	0
$\frac{1}{4}$ hour	2
$\frac{1}{2}$ hour	5
$\frac{3}{4}$ hour	4
1 hour	4

19. Use the table to complete the line plot.

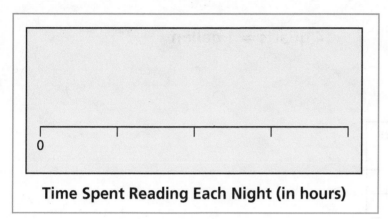

Time Spent Reading Each Night (in hours)

20. How many classmates did Jamal ask about time spent reading? _____

21. What amount of time had the most responses? _____

▶ Practice

Solve.

22. Fiona asked her friends how much time they spend using a computer at home each night. Use the information in the table to make a line plot.

Time Spent on Computer	Number of Students
0 hour	4
$\frac{1}{4}$ hour	4
$\frac{1}{2}$ hour	7
$\frac{3}{4}$ hour	3
1 hour	9

23. Marissa wants to know how many minutes she has practiced the piano. Label the double number line to show how hours and minutes are related. How many minutes has she practiced if she practiced for 4 hours?

_____

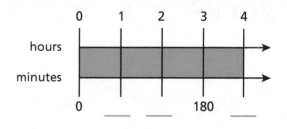

Name _____ Date _____

▶ Liquid Volume

In the customary system, the primary unit of
liquid volume is a **cup**.

1 cup 🥛 = 8 **fluid ounces**   4 cups 🥛🥛🥛🥛 = 1 **quart**

2 cups 🥛🥛 = 1 **pint**   4 quarts = 1 **gallon**

15. Complete the table.

Quarts	Fluid Ounces
1	32
2	
3	
4	
5	
6	

16. Label the double number line to show how gallons (gal)
and cups (c) are related.

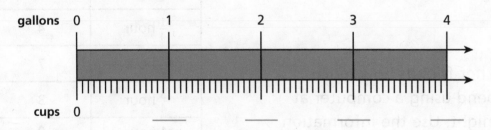

gallons 0   1   2   3   4

cups 0   ____   ____

Solve.

17. 3 qt = _____ c   **18.** 10 c = _____ fl oz   **19.** 2 gal = _____ pt

Name _____   Date _____

1. A photograph is 8 centimeters wide. After Kari enlarges the photograph, it is 3 times as wide as the original. How wide is the new photograph in millimeters?

_____ millimeters

2. Describe the relationship between these units of time: hours, minutes, and seconds.

3. Complete the table that relates meters and centimeters.

Meters	Centimeters
1	_____
2	_____
3	300
4	_____

4. What is the area of the rectangle?

17 m

5 m

_____ square meters

5. Classify the conversion below as using × 10, × 100, or × 1,000. Write the letter of the conversion in the correct box.

Ⓐ kilograms to grams   Ⓓ hectograms to decagrams

Ⓑ meters to centimeters   Ⓔ liters to milliliters

Ⓒ deciliters to centiliters   Ⓕ decameters to decimeters

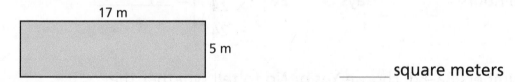

× 10	× 100	× 1,000

6. Write the length and width of the rectangle. Then write the perimeter. Be sure to choose the correct unit, inches or square inches, for each answer.

13 in.

12 in.

Length: ☐ ☐

Width: ☐ ☐

Perimeter: ☐ ☐

7. For numbers 7a and 7b, complete the conversion. Then choose the operation and complete the equation to show how you found your answer.

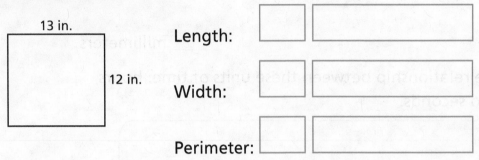

7a. 12 min = ☐ sec   12 | × 60 ÷ 60 × 24 ÷ 24 | = _____

7b. 96 hours = ☐ days   96 | × 60 ÷ 60 × 24 ÷ 24 | = _____

8. For numbers 8a–8d, choose Yes or No to tell whether the conversion between the metric units is correct.

8a. Divide by 100 to convert kiloliters to decaliters. ○ Yes   ○ No

8b. Multiply by 10 to convert milligrams to centigrams. ○ Yes   ○ No

8c. Divide by 1,000 to convert grams to kilograms. ○ Yes   ○ No

8d. Divide by 10 to convert kilometers to hectometers. ○ Yes   ○ No

9. Find the perimeter and area of the rectangle.

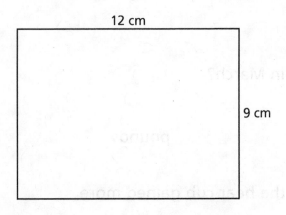

12 cm

9 cm

$P =$ ☐ centimeters

$A =$ ☐ square centimeters

10. Draw a line to match equivalent measurements.

48 inches	9 tons	24 cups	18 pounds
•	•	•	•

•	•	•	•
18,000 pounds	288 ounces	4 feet	192 fluid ounces

11. During a speech, a motivational speaker says, "There are 1,440 seconds in each day. How will you spend yours?"
Do you agree or disagree with the speaker? Explain your reasoning using words and numbers.

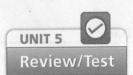
12. A bear cub weighs 64 ounces in March. After three months, it weighs 31 pounds.

Part A

How many pounds did the cub weigh in March?

_____ pounds

Part B

Use words and numbers to show that the bear cub gained more than 25 pounds after three months.

13. Jill asked her classmates how many hours of sleep they got last night. She displayed the data in the line plot shown. How many classmates did Jill ask about the time spent sleeping?

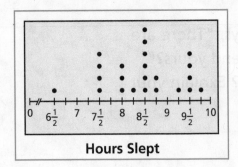

Hours Slept

Jill asked ☐ classmates.

14. Which mass is equivalent to 55 decagrams? Mark all that apply.

(A) 55 kilograms

(D) 5 hectograms

(B) 550 grams

(E) 550,000 milligrams

(C) 5,500 centigrams

(F) 55,000 decigrams

15. A rectangular scarf has an area of 192 square inches.
The short sides of the scarf are each 6 inches long.

Part A

Use the labels from the list to complete the model.
Labels can be used more than once.

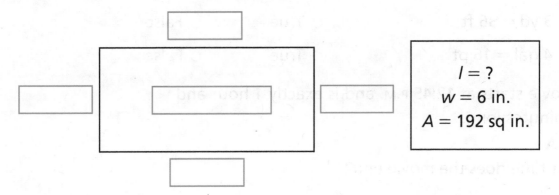

$l = ?$
$w = 6$ in.
$A = 192$ sq in.

Part B

What is the perimeter of the scarf? Show your work.

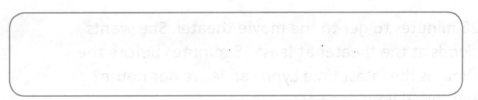

16. A rectangular cafeteria tray measures 18 inches on the
long sides. It measures 12 inches on the short sides.
What is the perimeter of the tray?

_____ inches

17. A bag of rice has a mass of 3 kilograms. Jackie buys 17 bags
of rice for the school cafeteria. How many grams of rice did
Jackie buy? Explain how you solved this problem.

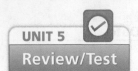
18. For numbers 18a–18e, choose True or False for the conversion.

    18a. 8 ft = 96 in.   ○ True   ○ False

    18b. 9 lb = 72 oz   ○ True   ○ False

    18c. 8 pt = 4 qt   ○ True   ○ False

    18d. 3 yd = 36 ft   ○ True   ○ False

    18e. 4 gal = 16 pt   ○ True   ○ False

19. A movie starts at 12:45 P.M. and is exactly 1 hour and 35 minutes long.

Part A

What time does the movie end?

Part B

It takes Lynn 25 minutes to get to the movie theater. She wants to meet her friends at the theater at least 15 minutes before the movie starts. What is the latest time Lynn can leave her house? Explain how you found your answer.

20. Choose a number from the first column and a unit from the second column to make a measurement that is equivalent to 2 meters.

Number	Unit
○ 100	○ decimeters
○ 20,000	○ centimeters
○ 200	○ millimeters

Family Letter

Content Overview

Dear Family,

Your child has experience with fractions through measurements and in previous grades. Unit 6 of *Math Expressions* builds on this experience. The main goals of this unit are to:

- understand the meaning of fractions.
- compare unit fractions.
- add and subtract fractions and mixed numbers with like denominators.
- multiply a fraction by a whole number.

Your child will use fraction bars and fraction strips to gain a visual and conceptual understanding of fractions as parts of a whole. Later, your child will use these models to add and subtract fractions and to convert between improper fractions and mixed numbers.

Examples of Fraction Bar Modeling:

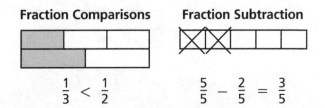

Fraction Comparisons

$$\frac{1}{3} < \frac{1}{2}$$

Fraction Subtraction

$$\frac{5}{5} - \frac{2}{5} = \frac{3}{5}$$

In later lessons of this unit, your child will be introduced to the number line model for fractions. Students name fractions corresponding to given lengths on the number line and identify lengths corresponding to given fractions. They also see that there are many equivalent fraction names for any given length.

Your child will apply this knowledge about fractions and fraction operations to solve real world problems.

If you have questions or problems, please contact me.

Sincerely,
Your child's teacher

© Houghton Mifflin Harcourt Publishing Company

 CA CC

Unit 6 addresses the following standards from the *Common Core Standards for Mathematics with California Additions*: 4.NF.3, 4.NF.3a, 4.NF.3b, 4.NF.3c, 4.NF.3d, 4.NF.4a, 4.NF.4b, 4.NF.4c, and all Mathematical Practices.

Un vistazo general al contenido

Estimada familia:

Su niño ha usado fracciones al hacer mediciones y en los grados previos. La Unidad 6 de *Math Expressions* amplía esta experiencia. Los objetivos principales de la unidad son:

- comprender el significado de las fracciones.
- comparar fracciones unitarias.
- sumar y restar fracciones y números mixtos con denominadores iguales.
- multiplicar una fracción por un número entero.

Su niño usará barras y tiras de fracciones para comprender y visualizar el concepto de las fracciones como partes de un entero. Luego, usará estos modelos para sumar y restar fracciones y para convertir fracciones impropias y números mixtos.

Ejemplos de modelos con barras de fracciones:

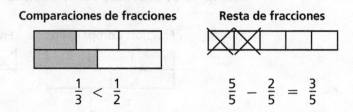

Comparaciones de fracciones

$$\frac{1}{3} < \frac{1}{2}$$

Resta de fracciones

$$\frac{5}{5} - \frac{2}{5} = \frac{3}{5}$$

Más adelante en esta unidad, su niño verá el modelo de la recta numérica para las fracciones. Los estudiantes nombrarán las fracciones que correspondan a determinadas longitudes en la recta numérica e identificarán longitudes que corresponden a fracciones dadas. También observarán que hay muchos nombres de fracciones equivalentes para una longitud determinada.

Su niño aplicará este conocimiento de las fracciones y operaciones con fracciones para resolver problemas cotidianos.

Si tiene alguna duda o algún comentario, por favor comuníquese conmigo.

Atentamente,
El maestro de su niño

© Houghton Mifflin Harcourt Publishing Company

CA CC

En la Unidad 6 se aplican los siguientes estándares auxiliares, contendidos en los *Estándares estatales comunes de matemáticas con adiciones para California*: **4.NF.3, 4.NF.3a, 4.NF.3b, 4.NF.3c, 4.NF.3d, 4.NF.4a, 4.NF.4b, 4.NF.4c** y todos los de prácticas matemáticas.

Name _____   Date _____

▶ Sums of Unit Fractions

Shade the fraction bar to show each fraction. Then write the fraction as a sum of unit fractions and as a product of a whole number and a unit fraction. The first one is done for you.

9. $\frac{3}{4}$ = $\frac{1}{4} + \frac{1}{4} + \frac{1}{4}$ = $3 \times \frac{1}{4}$

$\frac{1}{4}$	$\frac{1}{4}$	$\frac{1}{4}$	$\frac{1}{4}$

10. $\frac{3}{8}$ = _____ = _____

$\frac{1}{8}$	$\frac{1}{8}$	$\frac{1}{8}$	$\frac{1}{8}$	$\frac{1}{8}$	$\frac{1}{8}$	$\frac{1}{8}$	$\frac{1}{8}$

11. $\frac{5}{5}$ = _____ = _____

$\frac{1}{5}$	$\frac{1}{5}$	$\frac{1}{5}$	$\frac{1}{5}$	$\frac{1}{5}$

12. $\frac{2}{12}$ = _____ = _____

$\frac{1}{12}$	$\frac{1}{12}$	$\frac{1}{12}$	$\frac{1}{12}$	$\frac{1}{12}$	$\frac{1}{12}$	$\frac{1}{12}$	$\frac{1}{12}$	$\frac{1}{12}$	$\frac{1}{12}$	$\frac{1}{12}$	$\frac{1}{12}$

13. $\frac{4}{7}$ = _____ = _____

$\frac{1}{7}$	$\frac{1}{7}$	$\frac{1}{7}$	$\frac{1}{7}$	$\frac{1}{7}$	$\frac{1}{7}$	$\frac{1}{7}$

14. $\frac{7}{9}$ = _____ = _____

$\frac{1}{9}$	$\frac{1}{9}$	$\frac{1}{9}$	$\frac{1}{9}$	$\frac{1}{9}$	$\frac{1}{9}$	$\frac{1}{9}$	$\frac{1}{9}$	$\frac{1}{9}$

CA CC Content Standards 4.NF.2, 4.NF.3, 4.NF.3a, 4.NF.3b
Mathematical Practices MP.2, MP.3, MP.6

Name _____ Date _____

▶ Fifths that Add to One

Every afternoon, student volunteers help the school librarian put returned books back on the shelves. The librarian puts the books in equal piles on a cart.

One day, Jean and Maria found 5 equal piles on the return cart. They knew there were different ways they could share the job of reshelving the books. They drew fraction bars to help them find all the possibilities.

1. On each fifths bar, circle two groups of fifths to show one way Jean and Maria could share the work. (Each bar should show a different possibility.) Then complete the equation next to each bar to show their shares.

1 whole = all of the books

$\frac{1}{5}$	$\frac{1}{5}$	$\frac{1}{5}$	$\frac{1}{5}$	$\frac{1}{5}$

1 whole   Jean's share   Maria's share

$$\frac{5}{5} = \frac{}{5} + \frac{}{5}$$

$\frac{1}{5}$	$\frac{1}{5}$	$\frac{1}{5}$	$\frac{1}{5}$	$\frac{1}{5}$

$$\frac{5}{5} = \frac{}{5} + \frac{}{5}$$

$\frac{1}{5}$	$\frac{1}{5}$	$\frac{1}{5}$	$\frac{1}{5}$	$\frac{1}{5}$

$$\frac{5}{5} = \frac{}{5} + \frac{}{5}$$

$\frac{1}{5}$	$\frac{1}{5}$	$\frac{1}{5}$	$\frac{1}{5}$	$\frac{1}{5}$

$$\frac{5}{5} = \frac{}{5} + \frac{}{5}$$

Fractions that Add to One

▶ Sixths that Add to One

The librarian put 6 equal piles of returned books on the cart for Liu and Henry to reshelve. They also drew fraction bars.

2. On each sixths bar, circle two groups of sixths to show one way that Liu and Henry could share the work. (Each bar should show a different possibility.) Then complete the equation next to each bar to show their shares.

1 whole = all of the books

| $\frac{1}{6}$ | $\frac{1}{6}$ | $\frac{1}{6}$ | $\frac{1}{6}$ | $\frac{1}{6}$ | $\frac{1}{6}$ |

1 whole   Liu's   Henry's
       share   share

$\frac{6}{6} = \frac{}{6} + \frac{}{6}$

| $\frac{1}{6}$ | $\frac{1}{6}$ | $\frac{1}{6}$ | $\frac{1}{6}$ | $\frac{1}{6}$ | $\frac{1}{6}$ |

$\frac{6}{6} = \frac{}{6} + \frac{}{6}$

| $\frac{1}{6}$ | $\frac{1}{6}$ | $\frac{1}{6}$ | $\frac{1}{6}$ | $\frac{1}{6}$ | $\frac{1}{6}$ |

$\frac{6}{6} = \frac{}{6} + \frac{}{6}$

| $\frac{1}{6}$ | $\frac{1}{6}$ | $\frac{1}{6}$ | $\frac{1}{6}$ | $\frac{1}{6}$ | $\frac{1}{6}$ |

$\frac{6}{6} = \frac{}{6} + \frac{}{6}$

| $\frac{1}{6}$ | $\frac{1}{6}$ | $\frac{1}{6}$ | $\frac{1}{6}$ | $\frac{1}{6}$ | $\frac{1}{6}$ |

$\frac{6}{6} = \frac{}{6} + \frac{}{6}$

▶ Find the Unknown Addend

Write the fraction that will complete each equation.

3. $1 = \frac{7}{7} = \frac{1}{7} + \underline{\hspace{1cm}}$

4. $1 = \frac{4}{4} = \frac{3}{4} + \underline{\hspace{1cm}}$

5. $1 = \frac{8}{8} = \frac{3}{8} + \underline{\hspace{1cm}}$

6. $1 = \frac{5}{5} = \frac{2}{5} + \underline{\hspace{1cm}}$

7. $1 = \frac{3}{3} = \frac{2}{3} + \underline{\hspace{1cm}}$

8. $1 = \frac{10}{10} = \frac{6}{10} + \underline{\hspace{1cm}}$

9. $1 = \frac{6}{6} = \frac{2}{6} + \underline{\hspace{1cm}}$

10. $1 = \frac{8}{8} = \frac{5}{8} + \underline{\hspace{1cm}}$

Name _____ Date _____

CA CC Content Standards 4.NF.3a, 4.NF.3d, 4.MD.2
Mathematical Practices MP.2, MP.3, MP.4, MP.6

▶ Add Fractions

The circled parts of this fraction bar show an addition problem.

$\frac{1}{7}$	$\frac{1}{7}$	$\frac{1}{7}$	$\frac{1}{7}$	$\frac{1}{7}$	$\frac{1}{7}$	$\frac{1}{7}$

1. Write the numerators that will complete the addition equation.

$$\frac{}{7} + \frac{}{7} = \frac{+}{7} = \frac{}{7}$$

Solve each problem. Write the correct numerator to complete each equation.

2. $\frac{3}{9} + \frac{4}{9} = \frac{+}{9} = \frac{}{9}$

3. $\frac{1}{5} + \frac{3}{5} = \frac{+}{5} = \frac{}{5}$

4. $\frac{2}{8} + \frac{5}{8} = \frac{+}{8} = \frac{}{8}$

5. What happens to the numerators in each problem?

_____

6. What happens to the denominators in each problem?

_____

▶ Subtract Fractions

The circled and crossed-out parts of this fraction bar show a subtraction problem.

$\frac{1}{7}$	$\frac{1}{7}$	$\frac{1}{7}$	$\frac{1}{7}$	$\frac{1}{7}$	$\frac{1}{7}$	$\frac{1}{7}$

7. Write the numerators that will complete the subtraction equation.

$$\frac{}{7} - \frac{}{7} = \frac{-}{7} = \frac{}{7}$$

Add and Subtract Fractions with Like Denominators

▶ Fractions Bars

| one whole | | | | | | | | | | | | $\frac{1}{1}$ |

| $\frac{1}{2}$ | | | | | | $\frac{1}{2}$ | | | | | | $\frac{2}{2}$ |

| $\frac{1}{3}$ | | | | $\frac{1}{3}$ | | | | $\frac{1}{3}$ | | | | $\frac{3}{3}$ |

| $\frac{1}{4}$ | | | $\frac{1}{4}$ | | | $\frac{1}{4}$ | | | $\frac{1}{4}$ | | | $\frac{4}{4}$ |

| $\frac{1}{5}$ | | $\frac{1}{5}$ | | $\frac{1}{5}$ | | $\frac{1}{5}$ | | $\frac{1}{5}$ | | | | $\frac{5}{5}$ |

| $\frac{1}{6}$ | $\frac{1}{6}$ | $\frac{1}{6}$ | $\frac{1}{6}$ | $\frac{1}{6}$ | $\frac{1}{6}$ | | | | | | | $\frac{6}{6}$ |

| $\frac{1}{7}$ | $\frac{1}{7}$ | $\frac{1}{7}$ | $\frac{1}{7}$ | $\frac{1}{7}$ | $\frac{1}{7}$ | $\frac{1}{7}$ | | | | | | $\frac{7}{7}$ |

| $\frac{1}{8}$ | $\frac{1}{8}$ | $\frac{1}{8}$ | $\frac{1}{8}$ | $\frac{1}{8}$ | $\frac{1}{8}$ | $\frac{1}{8}$ | $\frac{1}{8}$ | | | | | $\frac{8}{8}$ |

| $\frac{1}{9}$ | $\frac{1}{9}$ | $\frac{1}{9}$ | $\frac{1}{9}$ | $\frac{1}{9}$ | $\frac{1}{9}$ | $\frac{1}{9}$ | $\frac{1}{9}$ | $\frac{1}{9}$ | | | | $\frac{9}{9}$ |

| $\frac{1}{10}$ | $\frac{1}{10}$ | $\frac{1}{10}$ | $\frac{1}{10}$ | $\frac{1}{10}$ | $\frac{1}{10}$ | $\frac{1}{10}$ | $\frac{1}{10}$ | $\frac{1}{10}$ | $\frac{1}{10}$ | | | $\frac{10}{10}$ |

| $\frac{1}{12}$ | $\frac{1}{12}$ | $\frac{1}{12}$ | $\frac{1}{12}$ | $\frac{1}{12}$ | $\frac{1}{12}$ | $\frac{1}{12}$ | $\frac{1}{12}$ | $\frac{1}{12}$ | $\frac{1}{12}$ | $\frac{1}{12}$ | $\frac{1}{12}$ | $\frac{12}{12}$ |

Add and Subtract Fractions with Like Denominators **79**

Add and Subtract Fractions with Like Denominators

▶ Understand Fractions Greater Than 1 and Mixed Numbers

1 whole

✂️

$\frac{1}{8}$	$\frac{1}{8}$	$\frac{1}{8}$	$\frac{1}{8}$	$\frac{1}{8}$	$\frac{1}{8}$	$\frac{1}{8}$	$\frac{1}{8}$
$\frac{1}{8}$	$\frac{1}{8}$	$\frac{1}{8}$	$\frac{1}{8}$	$\frac{1}{8}$	$\frac{1}{8}$	$\frac{1}{8}$	$\frac{1}{8}$
$\frac{1}{8}$	$\frac{1}{8}$	$\frac{1}{8}$	$\frac{1}{8}$	$\frac{1}{8}$	$\frac{1}{8}$	$\frac{1}{8}$	$\frac{1}{8}$
$\frac{1}{8}$	$\frac{1}{8}$	$\frac{1}{8}$	$\frac{1}{8}$	$\frac{1}{8}$	$\frac{1}{8}$	$\frac{1}{8}$	$\frac{1}{8}$
$\frac{1}{8}$	$\frac{1}{8}$	$\frac{1}{8}$	$\frac{1}{8}$	$\frac{1}{8}$	$\frac{1}{8}$	$\frac{1}{8}$	$\frac{1}{8}$
$\frac{1}{8}$	$\frac{1}{8}$	$\frac{1}{8}$	$\frac{1}{8}$	$\frac{1}{8}$	$\frac{1}{8}$	$\frac{1}{8}$	$\frac{1}{8}$
$\frac{1}{8}$	$\frac{1}{8}$	$\frac{1}{8}$	$\frac{1}{8}$	$\frac{1}{8}$	$\frac{1}{8}$	$\frac{1}{8}$	$\frac{1}{8}$

✂️

$\frac{1}{5}$	$\frac{1}{5}$	$\frac{1}{5}$	$\frac{1}{5}$	$\frac{1}{5}$
$\frac{1}{5}$	$\frac{1}{5}$	$\frac{1}{5}$	$\frac{1}{5}$	$\frac{1}{5}$
$\frac{1}{5}$	$\frac{1}{5}$	$\frac{1}{5}$	$\frac{1}{5}$	$\frac{1}{5}$
$\frac{1}{5}$	$\frac{1}{5}$	$\frac{1}{5}$	$\frac{1}{5}$	$\frac{1}{5}$
$\frac{1}{5}$	$\frac{1}{5}$	$\frac{1}{5}$	$\frac{1}{5}$	$\frac{1}{5}$
$\frac{1}{5}$	$\frac{1}{5}$	$\frac{1}{5}$	$\frac{1}{5}$	$\frac{1}{5}$
$\frac{1}{5}$	$\frac{1}{5}$	$\frac{1}{5}$	$\frac{1}{5}$	$\frac{1}{5}$

▶ Understand Fractions Greater Than 1 and Mixed Numbers (continued)

1 whole

1 whole
1 whole
1 whole
1 whole
1 whole
1 whole
1 whole

1 whole
1 whole
1 whole
1 whole
1 whole
1 whole
1 whole

Mixed Numbers and Fractions Greater Than 1

► **Practice Addition and Subtraction with Fractions Greater Than 1**

Add or subtract.

1. $\frac{8}{5} + \frac{3}{5} =$ _____

2. $\frac{6}{9} + \frac{12}{9} =$ _____

3. $\frac{10}{7} - \frac{3}{7} =$ _____

4. $\frac{10}{8} + \frac{7}{8} =$ _____

5. $\frac{9}{6} - \frac{4}{6} =$ _____

6. $\frac{19}{10} - \frac{7}{10} =$ _____

► **Add Mixed Numbers with Like Denominators**

Add.

7. $2\frac{3}{5}$
   $+ 1\frac{1}{5}$
   _____

8. $1\frac{2}{5}$
   $+ 3\frac{4}{5}$
   _____

9. $3\frac{5}{8}$
   $+ 1\frac{3}{8}$
   _____

10. $5\frac{2}{3}$
    $+ 2\frac{2}{3}$
    _____

► **Subtract Mixed Numbers with Like Denominators**

Subtract.

11. $5\frac{6}{8}$
    $- 3\frac{3}{8}$
    _____

12. $6\frac{2}{8}$
    $- 4\frac{5}{8}$
    _____

13. $4\frac{1}{5}$
    $- 1\frac{3}{5}$
    _____

14. $5\frac{1}{6}$
    $- 3\frac{4}{6}$
    _____

Explain each solution.

15. $\overset{5}{6}\overset{7+2=9}{\frac{2}{7}} = 5\frac{9}{7}$
    $- 1\frac{5}{7} = 1\frac{5}{7}$
    _____
    $4\frac{4}{7}$

16. $\overset{5}{6}\overset{6+2=8}{\frac{2}{6}} = 5\frac{8}{6}$
    $- 1\frac{5}{6} = 1\frac{5}{6}$
    _____
    $4\frac{3}{6}$

17. $\overset{5}{6}\overset{11+2=13}{\frac{2}{11}} = 5\frac{13}{11}$
    $- 1\frac{5}{11} = 1\frac{5}{11}$
    _____
    $4\frac{8}{11}$

_____

_____

_____

▶ Make a Line Plot

36. Make a mark anywhere on this line segment.

●————————————————————————————————————●

37. Measure the distance from the left end of the segment to your mark to the nearest quarter inch.

_____

38. Collect measurements from your classmates and record them in the line plot below.

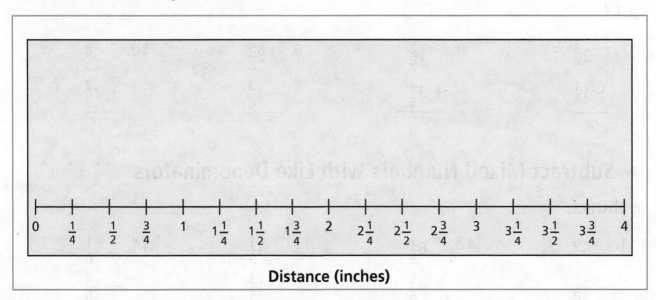

Distance (inches)

39. The range is the difference between the greatest value and the least value. What is the range of the data?

_____

40. Which distance value was most common?

_____

41. Describe any interesting patterns in the data values. For example, are there any large gaps? Are there clusters of values?

_____

_____

1. Represent the shaded part of the fraction bar as the product of a whole number and a unit fraction.

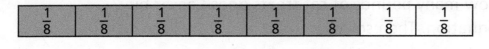

2. In the morning Naomi jumps rope for $\frac{1}{4}$ hour. After lunch she jumps rope for another $\frac{2}{4}$ hour. How long does Naomi jump rope? Write an equation. Then solve.

Equation: _____

Solution: _____ hour

3. For numbers 3a–3d, write a fraction from the tiles to make a true equation.

$$\boxed{\frac{1}{10}} \quad \boxed{\frac{2}{10}} \quad \boxed{\frac{3}{10}} \quad \boxed{\frac{4}{10}}$$

3a. $\frac{10}{10} = \frac{5}{10} + \frac{3}{10} + \boxed{}$

3c. $\frac{7}{10} = \frac{1}{10} + \frac{1}{10} + \frac{1}{10} + \frac{1}{10} + \boxed{}$

3b. $1 = \frac{1}{10} + \frac{5}{10} + \boxed{}$

3d. $\frac{4}{10} = \frac{1}{10} + \frac{1}{10} + \frac{1}{10} + \boxed{}$

4. Caesar buys dog treats and cat treats. He buys $\frac{7}{8}$ pound of dog treats. This is $\frac{5}{8}$ pound more than the weight of the cat treats he buys. How many pounds of cat treats does Caesar buy? Write an equation. Then solve.

   Equation: _____

   Solution: _____ pound

5. A recipe calls for $\frac{2}{3}$ cup of mushrooms. Dae uses 3 times as many cups of mushrooms. Choose the number of cups of mushrooms he uses. Mark all that apply.

   (A) $\frac{5}{3}$ cup

   (B) $\frac{6}{3}$ cups

   (C) 2 cups

   (D) 3 cups

6. Complete the table to show the fraction as a product of a whole number and a unit fraction.

Fraction	Product
$\frac{5}{12}$	_____
$\frac{2}{3}$	_____
$\frac{4}{7}$	_____

7. For 7a–7d, choose the operation that makes the equation true.

7a. $6 \begin{array}{c} + \\ - \\ \times \end{array} \frac{3}{4} = 4\frac{2}{4}$

7b. $3 \begin{array}{c} + \\ - \\ \times \end{array} \frac{2}{5} = 2\frac{3}{5}$

7c. $4 \begin{array}{c} + \\ - \\ \times \end{array} 3\frac{3}{5} = 7\frac{3}{5}$

7d. $7 \begin{array}{c} + \\ - \\ \times \end{array} \frac{1}{3} = 2\frac{1}{3}$

8. Multiply the expression to complete the table.

Expression	Written as a Fraction	Written as a Mixed Number
$7 \cdot \dfrac{1}{6}$	_____	_____
$12 \cdot \dfrac{1}{5}$	_____	$2\dfrac{2}{5}$
$3 \cdot \dfrac{5}{8}$	_____	_____

9. For numbers 9a–9f, choose True or False for the equation.

9a. $\dfrac{2}{8} + \dfrac{1}{8} = \dfrac{3}{16}$ ○ True   ○ False

9b. $\dfrac{4}{5} - \dfrac{1}{5} = \dfrac{3}{5}$ ○ True   ○ False

9c. $\dfrac{9}{4} + \dfrac{2}{4} = 2\dfrac{3}{4}$ ○ True   ○ False

9d. $\dfrac{5}{12} + \dfrac{4}{12} = \dfrac{9}{24}$ ○ True   ○ False

9e. $8\dfrac{5}{6} - 6\dfrac{4}{6} = 2\dfrac{1}{6}$ ○ True   ○ False

9f. $2\dfrac{7}{10} + 3\dfrac{3}{10} = 5\dfrac{10}{20}$ ○ True   ○ False

10. Elias says this problem can be solved using addition. Vladmir says it can be solved using multiplication. Explain why both boys are correct.

Milo practices piano $\dfrac{3}{5}$ hour every day. How many hours does he practice in 5 days?

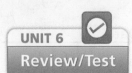
11. For 11a and 11b, find the sum or difference. Write your answer as a mixed number or a whole number, when possible.

11a. $\begin{array}{r} 5\frac{2}{3} \\ +\ 4\frac{2}{3} \\ \hline \end{array}$

11b. $\begin{array}{r} 9\frac{3}{8} \\ -\ 3\frac{7}{8} \\ \hline \end{array}$

12. On Saturday, Jesse plays basketball for $\frac{2}{3}$ hour. Then he plays some more. He plays $2\frac{1}{3}$ hours in all. How much longer did Jesse play basketball?

Part A

Draw a model to represent the problem. Then solve. Explain how your model helps you solve the problem.

Part B

On Sunday, Jesse played basketball for $1\frac{2}{3}$ hours. How many total hours did he play basketball on Saturday and Sunday? Show your work.

13. Rebecca's soup recipe calls for $\frac{3}{4}$ cup milk. She needs 3 times as much milk to make a triple batch of soup. How many cups of milk does Rebecca need?

Part A

Draw a model for the problem.

Part B

Use your model to write two equations for the problem. Then solve.

14. For numbers 14a–14e, choose Yes or No to tell whether the fraction is correctly expressed as the sum of other fractions.

14a. $\frac{8}{13} = \frac{5}{13} + \frac{3}{13}$ ○ Yes   ○ No

14b. $\frac{4}{5} = \frac{1}{5} + \frac{1}{5} + \frac{1}{5} + \frac{1}{5} + \frac{1}{5}$ ○ Yes   ○ No

14c. $\frac{6}{11} = \frac{4}{6} + \frac{2}{5}$ ○ Yes   ○ No

14d. $\frac{3}{8} = \frac{1}{8} + \frac{1}{8} + \frac{1}{8}$ ○ Yes   ○ No

14e. $\frac{10}{17} = \frac{5}{17} + \frac{5}{17}$ ○ Yes   ○ No

15. The line plot shows the lengths of trails Andrea hiked last month at a state park.

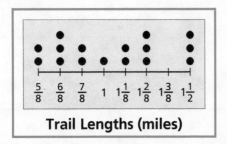

Trail Lengths (miles)

Andrea hiked 3 miles last week. She could have hiked two $1\frac{1}{2}$-mile trails. Describe two other combinations of trails she could have hiked.

16. Select the expression that is equivalent to $2\frac{2}{6}$. Mark all that apply.

Ⓐ $\frac{1}{6} + \frac{1}{6} + \frac{2}{6}$

Ⓓ $\frac{6}{6} + \frac{6}{6} + \frac{1}{6} + \frac{1}{6}$

Ⓑ $1 + 1 + \frac{2}{6}$

Ⓔ $\frac{20}{6} + \frac{2}{6}$

Ⓒ $\frac{2}{6} + \frac{2}{6} + \frac{2}{6}$

Ⓕ $\frac{6}{6} + \frac{3}{6} + \frac{3}{6} + \frac{2}{6}$

17. Explain how to change $\frac{11}{4}$ to a mixed number.

© Houghton Mifflin Harcourt Publishing Company

Family Letter

Content Overview

Dear Family,

In Lessons 1 through 7 of Unit 7 of *Math Expressions*, your child will build on previous experience with fractions. Your child will use both physical models and numerical methods to recognize and to find fractions equivalent to a given fraction. Your child will also compare fractions and mixed numbers, including those with like and unlike numerators and denominators.

By using fraction strips students determine how to model and compare fractions, and to find equivalent fractions. Your child will also learn how to use multiplication and division to find equivalent fractions.

Examples of Fraction Bar Modeling:

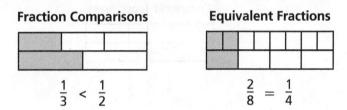

Fraction Comparisons

$$\frac{1}{3} < \frac{1}{2}$$

Equivalent Fractions

$$\frac{2}{8} = \frac{1}{4}$$

Your child will be introduced to the number-line model for fractions. Students name fractions corresponding to given lengths on the number line and identify lengths corresponding to given fractions. They also see that there are many equivalent fraction names for any given length.

Your child will apply this knowledge of fractions to word problems and in data displays.

If you have questions or problems, please contact me.

Thank you.

Sincerely,
Your child's teacher

 CA CC

Unit 7 addresses the following standards from the *Common Core State Standards for Mathematics with California Additions*: **4.NF.1, 4.NF.2, 4.NF.5, 4.MD.4,** and all Mathematical Practices.

Estimada familia:

En las lecciones 1 a 7 de la Unidad 7 de *Math Expressions*, el niño ampliará sus conocimientos previos acerca de las fracciones. Su niño usará modelos físicos y métodos numéricos para reconocer y hallar fracciones equivalentes para una fracción dada. También comparará fracciones y números mixtos, incluyendo aquellos que tengan numeradores y denominadores iguales o diferentes.

Usando tiras de fracciones, los estudiantes determinarán cómo hacer modelos y comparar fracciones y cómo hallar fracciones equivalentes. Además, aprenderán cómo usar la multiplicación y división para hallar fracciones equivalentes.

Ejemplos de modelos con barras de fracciones:

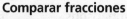
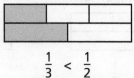
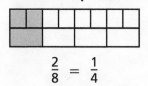

Comparar fracciones

$$\frac{1}{3} < \frac{1}{2}$$

Fracciones equivalentes

$$\frac{2}{8} = \frac{1}{4}$$

Su niño estudiará por primera vez el modelo de recta numérica para las fracciones. Los estudiantes nombrarán las fracciones que correspondan a determinadas longitudes en la recta numérica e identificarán longitudes que correspondan a fracciones dadas. También observarán que hay muchos nombres de fracciones equivalentes para una longitud determinada.

Su niño aplicará este conocimiento de las fracciones en problemas y en presentaciones de datos.

Si tiene alguna duda o algún comentario, por favor comuníquese conmigo.

Atentamente,
El maestro de su niño

 CA CC

En la Unidad 7 se aplican los siguientes estándares auxiliares, contenidos en los *Estándares estatales comunes de matemáticas con adiciones para California*: **4.NF.1, 4.NF.2, 4.NF.5, 4.MD.4** y todos los de prácticas matemáticas.

																			$\frac{1}{1}$

$\frac{1}{1}$

$\frac{1}{2}$ $\frac{1}{2}$ — $\frac{2}{2}$

$\frac{1}{3}$ $\frac{1}{3}$ $\frac{1}{3}$ — $\frac{3}{3}$

$\frac{1}{4}$ $\frac{1}{4}$ $\frac{1}{4}$ $\frac{1}{4}$ — $\frac{4}{4}$

$\frac{1}{5}$ $\frac{1}{5}$ $\frac{1}{5}$ $\frac{1}{5}$ $\frac{1}{5}$ — $\frac{5}{5}$

$\frac{1}{6}$ $\frac{1}{6}$ $\frac{1}{6}$ $\frac{1}{6}$ $\frac{1}{6}$ $\frac{1}{6}$ — $\frac{6}{6}$

$\frac{1}{7}$ $\frac{1}{7}$ $\frac{1}{7}$ $\frac{1}{7}$ $\frac{1}{7}$ $\frac{1}{7}$ $\frac{1}{7}$ — $\frac{7}{7}$

$\frac{1}{8}$ $\frac{1}{8}$ $\frac{1}{8}$ $\frac{1}{8}$ $\frac{1}{8}$ $\frac{1}{8}$ $\frac{1}{8}$ $\frac{1}{8}$ — $\frac{8}{8}$

$\frac{1}{9}$ $\frac{1}{9}$ $\frac{1}{9}$ $\frac{1}{9}$ $\frac{1}{9}$ $\frac{1}{9}$ $\frac{1}{9}$ $\frac{1}{9}$ $\frac{1}{9}$ — $\frac{9}{9}$

$\frac{1}{10}$ $\frac{1}{10}$ $\frac{1}{10}$ $\frac{1}{10}$ $\frac{1}{10}$ $\frac{1}{10}$ $\frac{1}{10}$ $\frac{1}{10}$ $\frac{1}{10}$ $\frac{1}{10}$ — $\frac{10}{10}$

$\frac{1}{11}$ $\frac{1}{11}$ $\frac{1}{11}$ $\frac{1}{11}$ $\frac{1}{11}$ $\frac{1}{11}$ $\frac{1}{11}$ $\frac{1}{11}$ $\frac{1}{11}$ $\frac{1}{11}$ $\frac{1}{11}$ — $\frac{11}{11}$

$\frac{1}{12}$ $\frac{1}{12}$ $\frac{1}{12}$ $\frac{1}{12}$ $\frac{1}{12}$ $\frac{1}{12}$ $\frac{1}{12}$ $\frac{1}{12}$ $\frac{1}{12}$ $\frac{1}{12}$ $\frac{1}{12}$ $\frac{1}{12}$ — $\frac{12}{12}$

$\frac{1}{13}$ $\frac{1}{13}$ $\frac{1}{13}$ $\frac{1}{13}$ $\frac{1}{13}$ $\frac{1}{13}$ $\frac{1}{13}$ $\frac{1}{13}$ $\frac{1}{13}$ $\frac{1}{13}$ $\frac{1}{13}$ $\frac{1}{13}$ $\frac{1}{13}$ — $\frac{13}{13}$

$\frac{1}{14}$ $\frac{1}{14}$ $\frac{1}{14}$ $\frac{1}{14}$ $\frac{1}{14}$ $\frac{1}{14}$ $\frac{1}{14}$ $\frac{1}{14}$ $\frac{1}{14}$ $\frac{1}{14}$ $\frac{1}{14}$ $\frac{1}{14}$ $\frac{1}{14}$ $\frac{1}{14}$ — $\frac{14}{14}$

$\frac{1}{15}$ $\frac{1}{15}$ $\frac{1}{15}$ $\frac{1}{15}$ $\frac{1}{15}$ $\frac{1}{15}$ $\frac{1}{15}$ $\frac{1}{15}$ $\frac{1}{15}$ $\frac{1}{15}$ $\frac{1}{15}$ $\frac{1}{15}$ $\frac{1}{15}$ $\frac{1}{15}$ $\frac{1}{15}$ — $\frac{15}{15}$

$\frac{1}{16}$ $\frac{1}{16}$ $\frac{1}{16}$ $\frac{1}{16}$ $\frac{1}{16}$ $\frac{1}{16}$ $\frac{1}{16}$ $\frac{1}{16}$ $\frac{1}{16}$ $\frac{1}{16}$ $\frac{1}{16}$ $\frac{1}{16}$ $\frac{1}{16}$ $\frac{1}{16}$ $\frac{1}{16}$ $\frac{1}{16}$ — $\frac{16}{16}$

$\frac{1}{17}$ $\frac{1}{17}$ $\frac{1}{17}$ $\frac{1}{17}$ $\frac{1}{17}$ $\frac{1}{17}$ $\frac{1}{17}$ $\frac{1}{17}$ $\frac{1}{17}$ $\frac{1}{17}$ $\frac{1}{17}$ $\frac{1}{17}$ $\frac{1}{17}$ $\frac{1}{17}$ $\frac{1}{17}$ $\frac{1}{17}$ $\frac{1}{17}$ — $\frac{17}{17}$

$\frac{1}{18}$ $\frac{1}{18}$ $\frac{1}{18}$ $\frac{1}{18}$ $\frac{1}{18}$ $\frac{1}{18}$ $\frac{1}{18}$ $\frac{1}{18}$ $\frac{1}{18}$ $\frac{1}{18}$ $\frac{1}{18}$ $\frac{1}{18}$ $\frac{1}{18}$ $\frac{1}{18}$ $\frac{1}{18}$ $\frac{1}{18}$ $\frac{1}{18}$ $\frac{1}{18}$ — $\frac{18}{18}$

$\frac{1}{19}$ $\frac{1}{19}$ $\frac{1}{19}$ $\frac{1}{19}$ $\frac{1}{19}$ $\frac{1}{19}$ $\frac{1}{19}$ $\frac{1}{19}$ $\frac{1}{19}$ $\frac{1}{19}$ $\frac{1}{19}$ $\frac{1}{19}$ $\frac{1}{19}$ $\frac{1}{19}$ $\frac{1}{19}$ $\frac{1}{19}$ $\frac{1}{19}$ $\frac{1}{19}$ $\frac{1}{19}$ — $\frac{19}{19}$

$\frac{1}{20}$ — $\frac{20}{20}$

Compare Fractions **93**

▶ Number Lines for Thirds and Sixths

Tell how many equal parts are between zero and 1.
Then write fraction labels above the equal parts.

6. _____

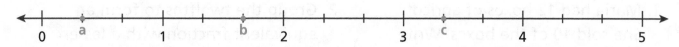

7. _____

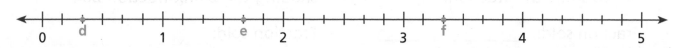

8. _____

Write > or < to make each statement true.

9. $\frac{4}{3}$ ◯ $\frac{7}{6}$

10. $\frac{8}{3}$ ◯ $\frac{18}{6}$

11. $3\frac{5}{6}$ ◯ $3\frac{2}{3}$

▶ Identify Points

12. Write the fraction or mixed number for each lettered
point above. Describe any patterns you see with the class.

a. _____   b. _____   c. _____

d. _____   e. _____   f. _____

g. _____   h. _____   i. _____

Mark and label the letter of each fraction or
mixed number on the number line.

13.

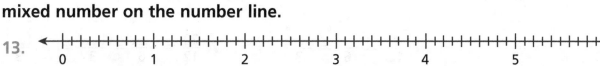

a. $\frac{1}{5}$ b. $\frac{7}{10}$ c. $1\frac{2}{5}$ d. $2\frac{1}{2}$

e. $3\frac{3}{10}$ f. $4\frac{2}{5}$ g. $4\frac{9}{10}$ h. $5\frac{1}{2}$

VOCABULARY
simplify

▶ Simplify Fractions

Simplifying a fraction means finding an equivalent fraction with a lesser numerator and denominator. Simplifying a fraction results in an equivalent fraction with fewer but greater unit fractions.

1. Maria had 12 boxes of apricots. She sold 10 of the boxes. Write the fraction of the boxes sold, and lightly shade the twelfths fraction bar to show this fraction.

   Fraction sold: _____

2. Group the twelfths to form an equivalent fraction with a lesser denominator. Show the new fraction by dividing, labeling, and lightly shading the blank fraction bar.

   Fraction sold: _____

$\frac{1}{12}$	$\frac{1}{12}$	$\frac{1}{12}$	$\frac{1}{12}$	$\frac{1}{12}$	$\frac{1}{12}$	$\frac{1}{12}$	$\frac{1}{12}$	$\frac{1}{12}$	$\frac{1}{12}$	$\frac{1}{12}$	$\frac{1}{12}$

3. In Problem 2, you formed groups of twelfths to get a greater unit fraction. How many twelfths are in each group? In other words, what is the *group size*?

   _____

4. Show how you can find the equivalent fraction by dividing the numerator and denominator by the group size.

   $$\frac{10}{12} = \frac{10 \div \square}{12 \div \square} = \frac{\square}{\square}$$

Use what you know to find these equivalent fractions. You may want to sketch a thirds fraction bar below the two fraction bars above.

5. $\dfrac{8}{12} = \dfrac{\square}{6} = \dfrac{\square}{3}$

6. $\dfrac{4}{12} = \dfrac{\square}{6} = \dfrac{\square}{3}$

7. $\dfrac{20}{12} = \dfrac{\square}{6} = \dfrac{\square}{3} = \square\dfrac{\square}{3}$

► Use Fraction Bars to Find Equivalent Fractions

8. Look at the thirds bar. Circle enough unit fractions on each of the other bars to equal $\frac{1}{3}$.

| $\frac{1}{18}$ | $\frac{1}{18}$ | $\frac{1}{18}$ | $\frac{1}{18}$ | $\frac{1}{18}$ | $\frac{1}{18}$ | $\frac{1}{18}$ | $\frac{1}{18}$ | $\frac{1}{18}$ | $\frac{1}{18}$ | $\frac{1}{18}$ | $\frac{1}{18}$ | $\frac{1}{18}$ | $\frac{1}{18}$ | $\frac{1}{18}$ | $\frac{1}{18}$ | $\frac{1}{18}$ | $\frac{1}{18}$ |

| $\frac{1}{15}$ | $\frac{1}{15}$ | $\frac{1}{15}$ | $\frac{1}{15}$ | $\frac{1}{15}$ | $\frac{1}{15}$ | $\frac{1}{15}$ | $\frac{1}{15}$ | $\frac{1}{15}$ | $\frac{1}{15}$ | $\frac{1}{15}$ | $\frac{1}{15}$ | $\frac{1}{15}$ | $\frac{1}{15}$ | $\frac{1}{15}$ |

| $\frac{1}{12}$ | $\frac{1}{12}$ | $\frac{1}{12}$ | $\frac{1}{12}$ | $\frac{1}{12}$ | $\frac{1}{12}$ | $\frac{1}{12}$ | $\frac{1}{12}$ | $\frac{1}{12}$ | $\frac{1}{12}$ | $\frac{1}{12}$ | $\frac{1}{12}$ |

| $\frac{1}{9}$ | $\frac{1}{9}$ | $\frac{1}{9}$ | $\frac{1}{9}$ | $\frac{1}{9}$ | $\frac{1}{9}$ | $\frac{1}{9}$ | $\frac{1}{9}$ | $\frac{1}{9}$ |

| $\frac{1}{6}$ | $\frac{1}{6}$ | $\frac{1}{6}$ | $\frac{1}{6}$ | $\frac{1}{6}$ | $\frac{1}{6}$ |

| $\frac{1}{3}$ | $\frac{1}{3}$ | $\frac{1}{3}$ |

9. Discuss how the parts of the fraction bars you circled show this chain of equivalent fractions. Explain how each different group of unit fractions is equal to $\frac{1}{3}$.

$$\frac{6}{18} = \frac{5}{15} = \frac{4}{12} = \frac{3}{9} = \frac{2}{6} = \frac{1}{3}$$

_____

_____

10. Write the group size for each fraction in the chain of equivalent fractions. The first one is done for you.

    6   _____   _____   _____   _____   _____

11. Complete each equation by showing how you use group size to simplify. The first one is done for you.

$$\frac{6 \div 6}{18 \div 6} = \frac{1}{3} \qquad \frac{5 \div \square}{15 \div \square} = \frac{1}{3} \qquad \frac{4 \div \square}{12 \div \square} = \frac{1}{3}$$

$$\frac{3 \div \square}{9 \div \square} = \frac{1}{3} \qquad \frac{2 \div \square}{6 \div \square} = \frac{1}{3}$$

► Make a Line Plot

Mai cut up strips of color paper to make a collage. The lengths of the unused pieces are shown in the table.

Length (in inches)	Number of Pieces
$\frac{1}{2}$	4
$\frac{5}{8}$	2
$\frac{3}{4}$	2
$\frac{7}{8}$	3
$1\frac{1}{4}$	2

7. Make a line plot to display the data.

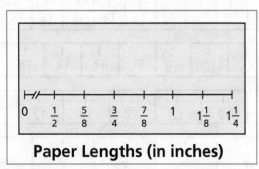

Paper Lengths (in inches)

8. Mai placed the shortest pieces in a row end to end. How long was the row?

_____

A group of students measured the widths of their hands. The measurements are shown in the table.

Width (in inches)	Number of Students
$2\frac{1}{4}$	1
$2\frac{3}{8}$	2
$2\frac{1}{2}$	2
$2\frac{5}{8}$	4
$2\frac{3}{4}$	2
$2\frac{7}{8}$	1

9. Make a line plot to display the data.

Hand Width (in inches)

10. What is the difference between the width of the widest hand and the most common hand width?

_____

11. Write a problem you could solve by using the line plot.

_____

_____

Fractions and Line Plots

Dear Family,

In this unit, your child will be introduced to decimal numbers. Students will begin by using what they already know about pennies, dimes, and dollars to see connections between fractions and decimals.

Students will explore decimal numbers by using bars divided into tenths and hundredths. They will relate decimals to fractions, which are also used to represent parts of a whole.

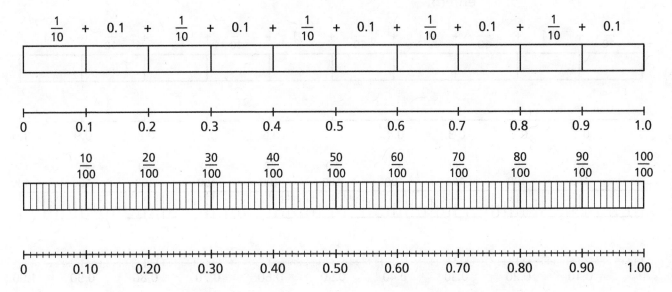

Students will read, write, and model decimal numbers. They will also learn to combine whole numbers with decimals. They will work with numbers such as 1.72 and 12.9. Students will also compare decimal numbers with other decimal numbers.

Students will apply their understanding of decimal concepts when they compare decimals.

Comparing Decimals

6.8 ◯ 3.42   6.80 ⟩ 3.42

Adding a zero makes the numbers easier to compare.

Please call if you have any questions or comments.

Thank you.

Sincerely,
Your child's teacher

 CA CC

Unit 7 addresses the following standards from the *Common Core State Standards for Mathematics with California Additions*: **4.NF.1, 4.NF.2, 4.NF.6, 4.NF.7, 4.MD.2, 4.MD.4,** and all Mathematical Practices.

Estimada familia:

En esta unidad, se presentarán los números decimales. Para comenzar, los estudiantes usarán lo que ya saben acerca de las monedas de un centavo, de las monedas de diez y de los dólares, para ver cómo se relacionan las fracciones y los decimales.

Los estudiantes estudiarán los números decimales usando barras divididas en décimos y centésimos. Relacionarán los decimales con las fracciones que también se usan para representar partes del entero.

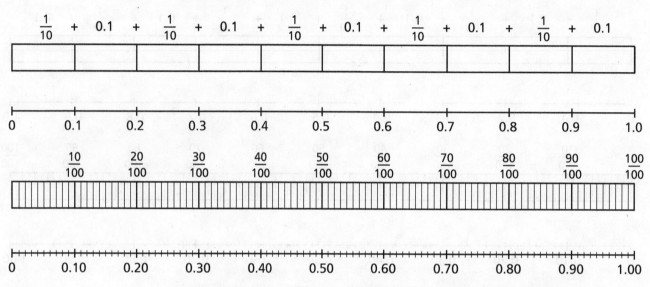

Los estudiantes leerán, escribirán y representarán números decimales. También aprenderán a combinar números enteros con decimales. Trabajarán con números tales como 1.72 y 12.9. Compararán números decimales con otros números decimales.

Al comparar decimales, los estudiantes aplicarán los conceptos decimales que ya conozcan.

Comparar decimales

$6.8 \bigcirc 3.42$ $6.80 \enclose{circle}{>} 3.42$

Añadir un cero facilita la comparación de números.

Si tiene alguna duda o algún comentario, por favor comuníquese conmigo.

Gracias.

Atentamente,
El maestro de su niño

 CA CC

En la Unidad 7 se aplican los siguientes estándares auxiliares, contenidos en los *Estándares estatales comunes de matemáticas con adiciones para California*: **4.NF.1, 4.NF.2, 4.NF.6, 4.NF.7, 4.MD.2, 4.MD.4** y todos los de prácticas matemáticas.

▶ Model Equivalent Fractions and Decimals

Write a fraction and a decimal to represent the shaded part of each whole.

15.

16.

Divide each whole and use shading to show the given fraction or decimal.

17.   0.75   18. $\frac{9}{10}$

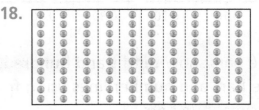

Shade these grids to show that $\frac{3}{2} = 1\frac{1}{2}$.

19.

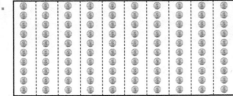   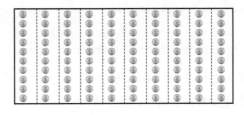

Name _____ **Date** _____

CA CC Content Standards **4.NF.6, 4.MD.2**
Mathematical Practices **MP.1, MP.2, MP.3, MP.6**

VOCABULARY
tenths
hundredths
decimal number

▶ Understand Tenths and Hundredths

Answer the questions about the bars and number lines below.

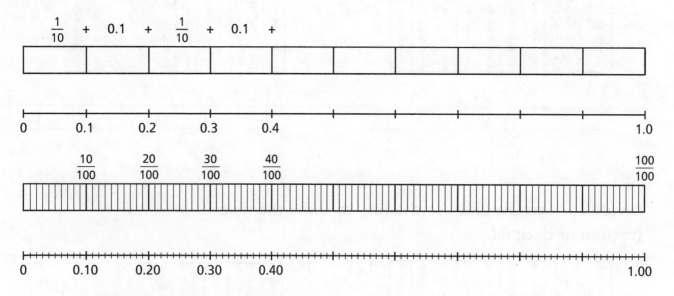

$\frac{1}{10}$ + 0.1 + $\frac{1}{10}$ + 0.1 +

0   0.1   0.2   0.3   0.4   1.0

$\frac{10}{100}$ $\frac{20}{100}$ $\frac{30}{100}$ $\frac{40}{100}$ $\frac{100}{100}$

0   0.10   0.20   0.30   0.40   1.00

1. The bars show **tenths** and **hundredths**. Finish labeling
   the bars and number lines using fractions and
   decimal numbers.

2. Use what you know about fractions and about money
   (a dime = one tenth of a dollar and a penny = one
   hundredth of a dollar) to explain why 3 tenths is the
   same as 30 hundredths.

   _____

   _____

3. Tenths are greater than hundredths even though 10 is
   less than 100. Explain why this is true.

   _____

   _____

Explore Decimal Numbers

► **Decimal Secret Code Cards**

0.1	0.01
0.2	0.02
0.3	0.03
0.4	0.04
0.5	0.05
0.6	0.06
0.7	0.07
0.8	0.08
0.9	0.09

.00

.00

.00

.00

> <

▶ Decimal Secret Code Cards

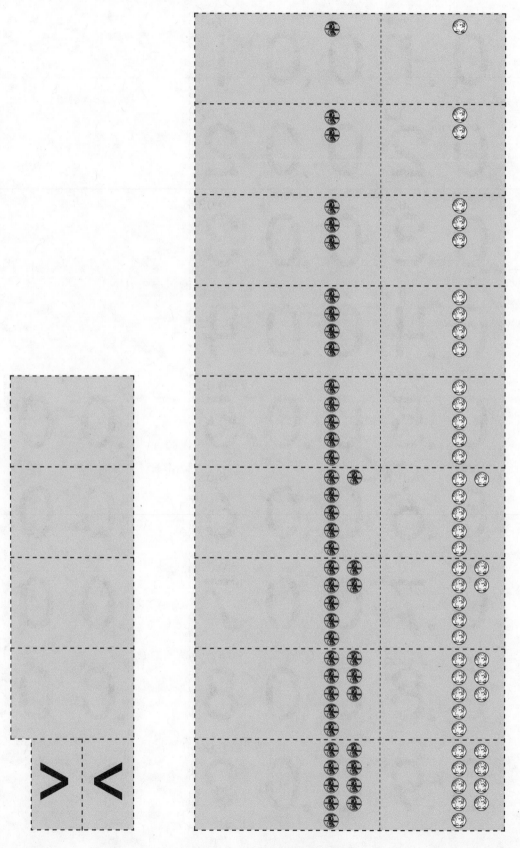

Decimal Secret Code Cards

Name _____ **Date** _____

CA CC Content Standards **4.NF.6, 4.MD.2**
Mathematical Practices **MP.1, MP.5, MP.7**

▶ Discuss Symmetry Around the Ones

$\times$ **10 (Greater)** $\div$ **10 (Lesser)**

Hundreds	Tens	ONES	Tenths	Hundredths
100.	10.	1.	0.1	0.01
$\frac{100}{1}$	$\frac{10}{1}$	$\frac{1}{1}$	$\frac{1}{10}$	$\frac{1}{100}$
$100.00	$10.00	$1.00	$0.10	$0.01

1. Discuss symmetries and relationships you see in the place value chart.

2. Is it easier to see place value patterns in **a** or **b**? Discuss why.

   a. 500   50   5   .5   .05

   b. 500   50   5   0.5   0.05

▶ Show and Read Decimal Numbers

Use your Decimal Secret Code Cards to make numbers on the frame.

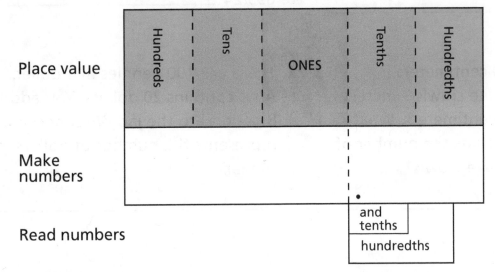

© Houghton Mifflin Harcourt Publishing Company

▶ Write Numbers in Decimal Form

Read and write each mixed number as a decimal.

3. $3\frac{1}{10}$ _____

4. $5\frac{7}{100}$ _____

5. $2\frac{46}{100}$ _____

6. $28\frac{9}{10}$ _____

Read and write each decimal as a mixed number.

7. 12.8 _____

8. 3.05 _____

9. 4.85 _____

10. 49.7 _____

Read each word name. Then write a decimal for each word name.

11. sixty-one hundredths

_____

12. six and fourteen hundredths

_____

13. seventy and eight tenths

_____

14. fifty-five and six hundredths

_____

▶ Expanded Form

Write each decimal in expanded form.

15. 8.2 _____

16. 17.45 _____

17. 106.24 _____

18. 50.77 _____

19. 312.09 _____

20. 693.24 _____

Solve.

21. There are 100 centimeters in 1 meter. A snake crawls 3 meters and 12 more centimeters. What decimal represents the number of meters the snake crawls?

_____

22. There are 100 pennies in 1 dollar. A jar contains 20 dollars. You add 8 pennies to the jar. What decimal represents the number of dollars in the jar?

_____

► Decimal Secret Code Cards

100		10		1
1	0 0	1	0	1
200		20		2
2	0 0	2	0	2
300		30		3
3	0 0	3	0	3
400		40		4
4	0 0	4	0	4
500		50		5
5	0 0	5	0	5
600		60		6
6	0 0	6	0	6
700		70		7
7	0 0	7	0	7
800		80		8
8	0 0	8	0	8
900		90		9
9	0 0	9	0	9

▶ Decimal Secret Code Cards

$1	$10	$100

© Houghton Mifflin Harcourt Publishing Company

Decimal Secret Code Cards

1. For numbers 1a–1d, write > or < to make the inequality true.

1a. $\frac{3}{5}$ ◯ $\frac{1}{5}$ 1c. $\frac{9}{10}$ ◯ $\frac{9}{12}$

1b. $\frac{2}{8}$ ◯ $\frac{2}{3}$ 1d. $\frac{5}{8}$ ◯ $\frac{7}{8}$

2. Choose numbers from the tiles to make an equivalent fraction with the least possible denominator.

| 2 | 3 | 4 | 6 |

$\frac{8}{12} = \dfrac{\boxed{}}{\boxed{}}$

3. Farid measures the masses of four books in kilograms. He records the data in the table. Which two books have the same mass?

Masses of Books				
Book	1	2	3	4
Mass (kg)	1.12	1.20	1.02	1.2

Ⓐ Books 1 and 3   Ⓒ Books 3 and 4

Ⓑ Books 2 and 3   Ⓓ Books 2 and 4

4. In a survey, $\frac{7}{10}$ of the students said they watched the news last week. Complete the fraction equation.

$\frac{7}{10} = \dfrac{\boxed{}}{100}$

5. A trail is $\frac{7}{12}$ mile long. Select the trail length that is shorter than $\frac{7}{12}$ mile. Mark all that apply.

   Ⓐ $\frac{3}{8}$ mile   Ⓒ $\frac{3}{4}$ mile

   Ⓑ $\frac{2}{3}$ mile   Ⓓ $\frac{1}{2}$ mile

6. On average, a chimpanzee spends about $\frac{2}{5}$ of the day sleeping. A squirrel spends about $\frac{5}{8}$ of the day sleeping. A three-toed sloth spends about $\frac{5}{6}$ of the day sleeping. For numbers 6a–6d, choose True or False to best describe the statement.

   6a. A chimpanzee spends more of the day
       sleeping than a three-toed sloth.   ○ True   ○ False

   6b. A squirrel spends more of the day
       sleeping than a chimpanzee.   ○ True   ○ False

   6c. A three-toed sloth spends more of
       the day sleeping than a squirrel.   ○ True   ○ False

   6d. A chimpanzee sleeps more than the
       other two types of animals.   ○ True   ○ False

7. Emily and Leah each brought a full water bottle to practice. Their bottles were the same except that Leah's bottle was taller than Emily's. Each girl drank $\frac{1}{2}$ of her water.

   Part A

   Draw a picture to show Emily and Leah's water bottles. Shade the bottles to show how much water each girl originally had. Then cross out the amount each girl drank.

   _____

   Part B

   Did each girl drink the same amount of water? Explain.

   _____

Name _____ **Date** _____

8. Locate and draw a point on the number line for the fraction or mixed number. Then label it with its corresponding letter.

a. $4\frac{1}{2}$ b. $\frac{7}{8}$ c. $1\frac{3}{4}$ d. $3\frac{1}{4}$ e. $2\frac{3}{8}$

9. For numbers 9a–9c, complete the chain of equivalent fractions.

9a. $\frac{2}{5} = \dfrac{\boxed{}}{10} = \dfrac{\boxed{}}{15} = \dfrac{\boxed{}}{20}$

9b. $\frac{6}{12} = \dfrac{\boxed{}}{6} = \dfrac{1}{\boxed{}}$

9c. $\frac{5}{8} = \dfrac{\boxed{}}{16} = \dfrac{\boxed{}}{24} = \dfrac{20}{\boxed{}}$

10. Write five fractions that are equivalent to $\frac{1}{6}$.

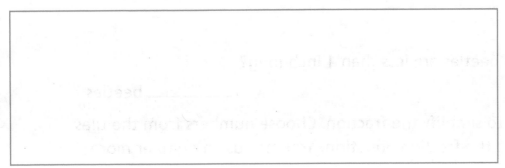

11. A lizard has a length of $\frac{43}{100}$ meter. Write $\frac{43}{100}$ in decimal form.

$\boxed{}$

12. Tione is researching beetles. She records the lengths of some beetles in the table.

Length (in inches)	Number of Beetles
$\frac{1}{4}$	2
$\frac{1}{2}$	3
$\frac{3}{4}$	6
1	1
$1\frac{1}{4}$	4
$1\frac{1}{2}$	2

Part A

Make a line plot to display the data.

Part B

How many beetles are less than 1 inch long?

_____ beetles

13. Show how to simplify the fraction. Choose numbers from the tiles to complete the fraction equation. You may use a number more than once.

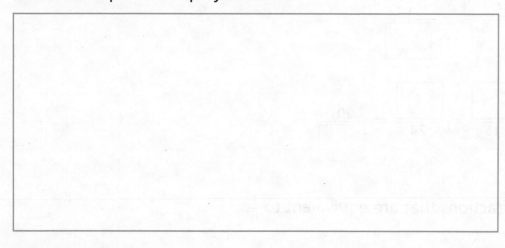

2	3
5	6

$$\frac{6}{10} = \frac{6 \div \boxed{}}{10 \div \boxed{}} = \frac{\boxed{}}{\boxed{}}$$

14. Write a decimal to make the statement true.

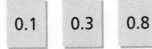

0.1   0.3   0.8

☐ > 0.65   0.15 > ☐   ☐ = 0.30

15. A forest ranger saw 10 deer. There were 2 male and 8 female
deer. What fraction or decimal number shows the part of the
deer that were female? Mark all that apply.

(A) $\frac{2}{10}$ (C) 0.80   (E) $\frac{8}{10}$

(B) 0.2   (D) 0.08   (F) 0.8

16. Each model represents 1 whole dollar. The shaded part represents
the part of a dollar Loren took to the bank.

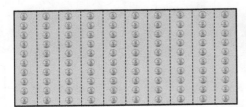   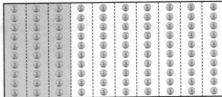

Part A

Write a mixed number to represent the part of a dollar Loren
took to the bank.

Part B

Loren says she can represent the part of a dollar she took to the
bank as 1.3 but not as 1.30. Do you agree? Why or why not?

17. Beth wrote the number sixty-one and twelve hundredths in decimal form. What did Beth write?

18. Trading cards come in packs of 100. Becca has 3 full packs and 7 more cards. For 18a–18d, choose Yes or No to tell whether the number represents the number of packs Becca has.

18a. 3.07   ○ Yes   ○ No

18b. 3 and 7 hundredths   ○ Yes   ○ No

18c. three and one seventh   ○ Yes   ○ No

18d. 3.7   ○ Yes   ○ No

19. A vet measures the mass of three puppies. Suzy's mass is 3.3 kilograms. Buster's mass is 3.03 kilograms, and Charlie's mass is 3.30 kilograms.

Part A

Is Suzy's mass the same as Charlie's? Explain.

Part B

A fourth puppy, Pluto, has a mass of 3.33 kilograms. Which of the four puppies has the least mass? Explain how you found your answer.

Dear Family,

In the first half of Unit 8, your child will be learning to recognize and describe geometric figures. One type of figure is an angle. Your child will use a protractor to find the measures of angles.

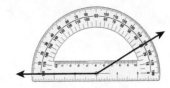

Other figures, such as triangles, may be named based on their angles and sides.

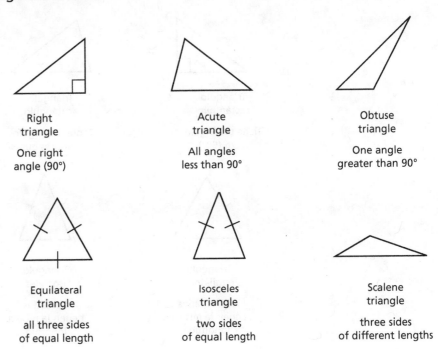

Right triangle	Acute triangle	Obtuse triangle
One right angle (90°)	All angles less than 90°	One angle greater than 90°

Equilateral triangle	Isosceles triangle	Scalene triangle
all three sides of equal length	two sides of equal length	three sides of different lengths

Be sure that your child continues to review and practice the basics of multiplication and division. A good understanding of the basics will be very important in later math courses when students learn more difficult concepts in multiplication and division.

If you have any questions or comments, please call or write to me.

Thank you.

Sincerely,
Your child's teacher

 CA CC

Unit 8 addresses the following standards from the *Common Core State Standards for Mathematics with California Additions*: **4.MD.5, 4.MD.5a, 4.MD.5b, 4.MD.6, 4.MD.7, 4.G.1, 4.G.2**, and all the Mathematical Practices.

Estimada familia:

En la primera parte de la Unidad 8, su niño aprenderá a reconocer y a describir figuras geométricas. Un ángulo es un tipo de figura. Su niño usará un transportador para hallar las medidas de los ángulos.

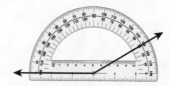

Otras figuras, tales como los triángulos, se nombran según sus ángulos y lados.

Triángulo rectángulo

Tiene un ángulo recto (90°)

Triángulo acutángulo

Todos los ángulos son menores que 90°

Triángulo obtusángulo

Tiene un ángulo mayor que 90°

Triángulo equilátero

los tres lados tienen la misma longitud

Triángulo isósceles

dos lados tienen la misma longitud

Triángulo escaleno

los tres lados tienen diferente longitud

Asegúrese de que su niño siga repasando y practicando las multiplicaciones y divisiones básicas. Es importante que domine las operaciones básicas para que, en los cursos de matemáticas de más adelante, pueda aprender conceptos de multiplicación y división más difíciles.

Si tiene alguna pregunta o algún comentario, por favor comuníquese conmigo.

Gracias.

Atentamente,
El maestro de su niño

© Houghton Mifflin Harcourt Publishing Company

CA CC

En la Unidad 8 se aplican los siguientes estándares auxiliares, contenidos en los *Estándares estatales comunes de matemáticas con adiciones para California*: **4.MD.5, 4.MD.5a, 4.MD.5b, 4.MD.6, 4.MD.7, 4.G.1, 4.G.2** y todos los de prácticas matemáticas.

▶ Drawing Points, Rays, and Angles

An **angle** is formed by two **rays** with the same endpoint, called the **vertex**.

You can label figures with letters to name them. This is ∠ABC. Its rays are $\overrightarrow{BA}$ and $\overrightarrow{BC}$.

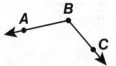

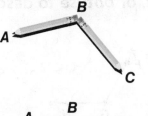

Draw and label each figure.

2. Draw and label a point. Write the name of your point. _____

3. Draw a ray. Label the endpoint. Write the name of your ray. _____

4. Draw an angle. Label the vertex and the two rays. Write the name of your angle. _____

▶ **Classify Angles**

Use the letters to name each angle. Then write *acute,*
right, **or** *obtuse* **to describe each angle.**

10.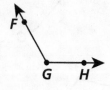

_____

_____

11.

_____

_____

12.

_____

_____

13. Use the letters to name two acute and two obtuse angles in
this figure. Write *acute* or *obtuse* to describe each angle.

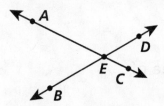

_____

_____

_____

_____

14. Draw and label a right angle, an acute angle, and
an obtuse angle.

▶ Sort Angles

Cut along the dashed lines.

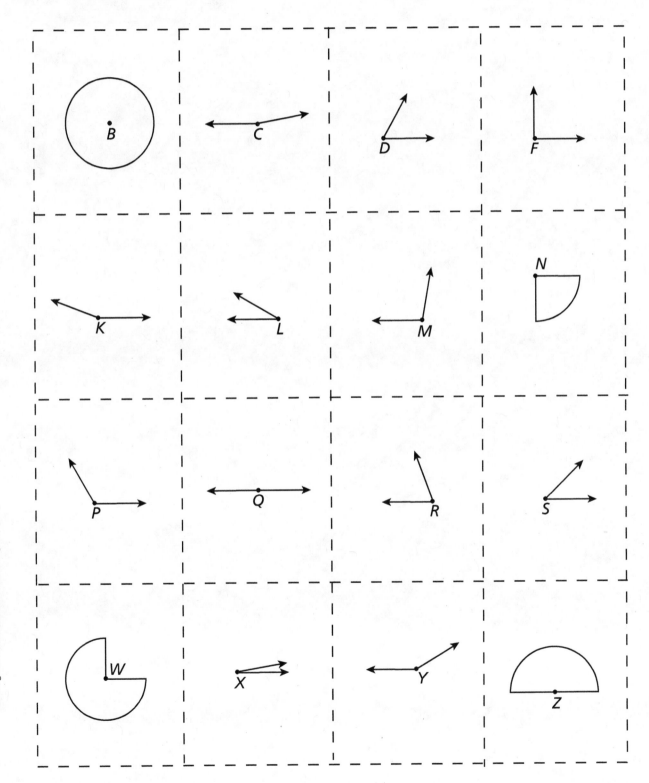

Points, Rays, and Angles

VOCABULARY
protractor

▶ Use a Protractor

A **protractor** is a tool that is used to measure angles in degrees. This protractor shows that ∠ABC measures 90°.

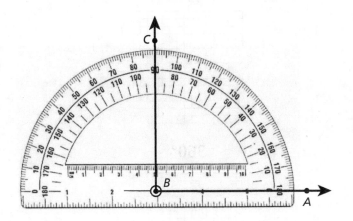

Measure each angle with your protractor. Write the measure.

1.

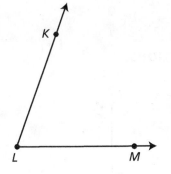

∠KLM = _____

2.

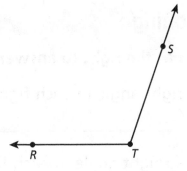

∠STR = _____

3.

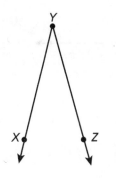

∠XYZ = _____

4.

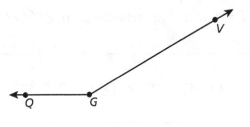

∠QGV = _____

▶ **Sketch Angles**

Sketch each angle, or draw it using a protractor.

5.   90°

6.   45°

7.   180°

8.   360°

▶ **Use Reasoning**

Use the figures at the right to answer the following questions.

9. Name one right angle in each figure.

_____

10. Name one straight angle in each figure.

_____

11. How much greater is the measure of ∠KRB than the measure of ∠IAO?

_____

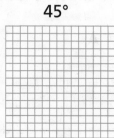

12. Which angle appears to be a 45° angle?

_____

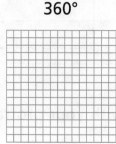

13. The measure of ∠IAE is 135°.

What is the measure of ∠OAE? _____

What is the measure of ∠UAE? _____

Measuring Angles

Name _____   Date _____

▶ Draw Angles in a Circle

Use a straightedge and a protractor to draw and shade an angle of each type. Measure and label each angle.

1. obtuse angle

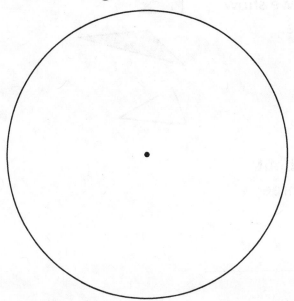

2. straight angle

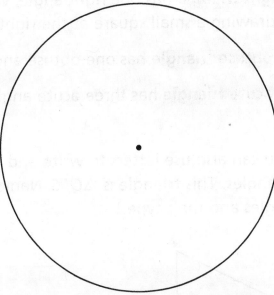

3. acute angle

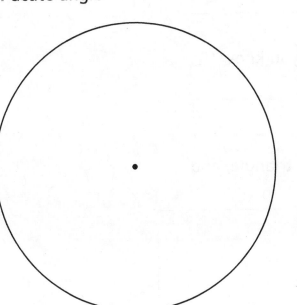

4. three angles with a sum of 360°

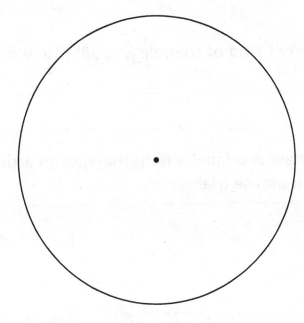

5. Write out the sum of your angle measures in Exercise 4 to show that it equals 360°

Name _____

Date _____

CA CC Content Standards **4.G.1, 4.G.2**
Mathematical Practices **MP.3, MP.5, MP.6, MP.7, MP.8**

▶ Discuss Angles of a Triangle

The prefix *tri-* means "three," so it is easy to remember that a triangle has 3 angles. Triangles can take their names from the kind of angles they have.

- A **right triangle** has one right angle, which we show by drawing a small square at the right angle.

- An **obtuse triangle** has one obtuse angle.

- An **acute triangle** has three acute angles.

1. You can also use letters to write and talk about triangles. This triangle is △*QRS*. Name its three angles and their type.

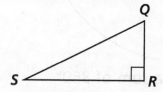

_____

_____

_____

2. What kind of triangle is △*QRS*? How do you know?

_____

_____

3. Draw and label a right triangle, an acute triangle, and an obtuse triangle.

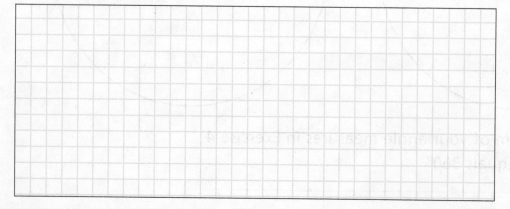

Name Triangles

▶ Sort Triangles in Different Ways

33. Write a capital letter and a lowercase letter inside each triangle below, using the keys at the right.

   Cut out the triangles and use the diagram below to sort them in different ways.

acute = a
obtuse = o
right = r

Isosceles = I
Scalene = S
Equilateral = E

Triangles

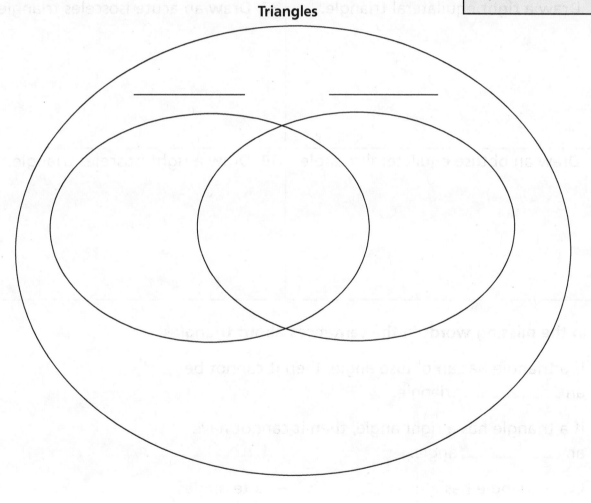

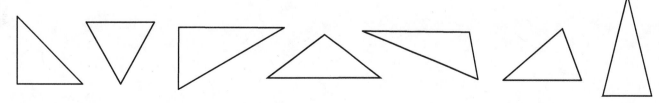

▶ Possible Ways to Name Triangles

Draw each triangle. If you can't, explain why.

34. Draw a right scalene triangle.	**35.** Draw an obtuse scalene triangle.
36. Draw a right equilateral triangle.	**37.** Draw an acute isosceles triangle.
38. Draw an obtuse equilateral triangle.	**39.** Draw a right isosceles triangle.

Fill in the missing words in the sentences about triangles.

40. If a triangle has an obtuse angle, then it cannot be
   an _____ triangle.

41. If a triangle has a right angle, then it cannot have
   an _____ angle.

42. Every triangle has at least _____ acute angles.

Dear Family,

Your child has been learning about geometry throughout this unit. In this second half of the unit, your child will be learning how to recognize and describe a group of geometric figures called quadrilaterals, which get their name because they have four (*quad-*) sides (*-lateral*). Five different kinds of quadrilaterals are shown here.

Square
4 equal sides
opposite sides parallel
4 right angles

Rectangle
2 pairs of parallel sides
4 right angles

Rhombus
4 equal sides
opposite sides parallel

Parallelogram
2 pairs of parallel sides

Trapezoid
exactly 1 pair of opposite sides parallel

If you have any questions or comments, please call or write to me.

Sincerely,
Your child's teacher

 CA CC

Unit 8 addresses the following standards from the *Common Core State Standards for Mathematics with California Additions*: **4.OA.5, 4.G.1, 4.G.2, 4.G.3**, and all the Mathematical Practices.

Estimada familia:

Durante esta unidad, su niño ha estado aprendiendo acerca de geometría. En esta parte de la unidad, su niño aprenderá cómo reconocer y describir un grupo de figuras geométricas llamadas cuadriláteros, que reciben ese nombre porque tienen cuatro *(quadri-)* lados *(-lateris)*. Aquí se muestran cinco tipos de cuadriláteros:

Cuadrado
4 lados iguales
lados opuestos paralelos
4 ángulos rectos

Rectángulo
2 pares de lados paralelos
4 ángulos rectos

Rombo
4 lados iguales
lados opuestos paralelos

Paralelogramo
2 pares de lados paralelos

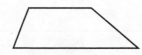

Trapecio
exactamente 1 par de lados paralelos opuestos

Si tiene alguna pregunta o algún comentario, por favor comuníquese conmigo.

Atentamente,
El maestro de su niño

 CA CC

En la Unidad 8 se aplican los siguientes estándares auxiliares, contenidos en los *Estándares estatales comunes de matemáticas con adiciones para California*: **4.OA.5, 4.G.1, 4.G.2, 4.G.3** y todos los de prácticas matemáticas.

▶ Define Parallel Lines

The lines or line segments in these pairs are **parallel**.

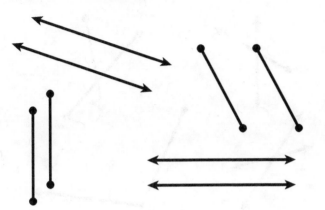

The lines or line segments in these pairs are not parallel.

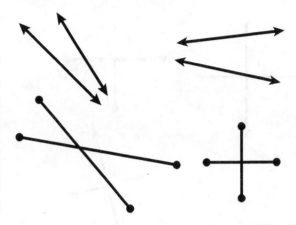

1. What do you think it means for two lines to be parallel?

_____

_____

▶ Draw Parallel Lines

2. Draw and label a pair of parallel lines.

3. Draw and label a figure with one pair of parallel line segments.

► Define Perpendicular Lines

The lines or line segments in these pairs are **perpendicular**.

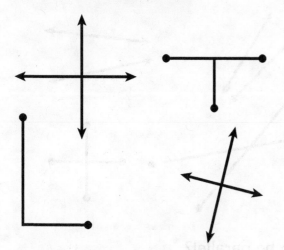

The lines or line segments in these pairs are not perpendicular.

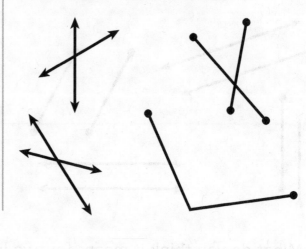

4. What do you think it means for two lines to be perpendicular?

► Draw Perpendicular Lines

5. Draw and label a pair of perpendicular lines.

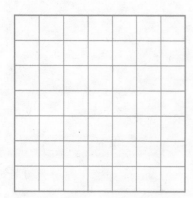

6. Draw and label a figure with one pair of perpendicular line segments.

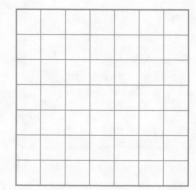

▶ Draw Special Quadrilaterals

5. Draw a quadrilateral that has exactly one pair of opposite sides parallel. What type of quadrilateral is it?

_____

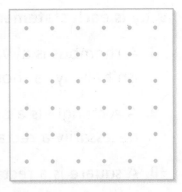

6. Draw a quadrilateral that has two pairs of opposite sides parallel. What type of quadrilateral is it? Is there more than one answer?

_____

7. Draw a quadrilateral that has two pairs of opposite sides parallel, 4 equal sides, and no right angles. What type of quadrilateral is it?

_____

► Identify Relationships

Why is each statement below true?

8. A rhombus is always a parallelogram, but a parallelogram isn't always a rhombus.

9. A rectangle is a parallelogram, but a parallelogram is not necessarily a rectangle.

10. A square is a rectangle, but a rectangle does not have to be a square.

11. Complete the category diagram by placing each word in the best location.

   Quadrilateral
   Trapezoid
   Parallelogram
   Rectangle
   Rhombus
   Square

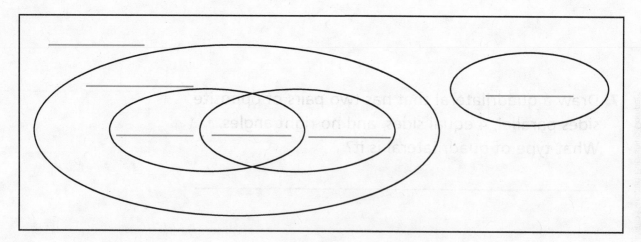

Classify Quadrilaterals

▶ Sort and Classify Quadrilaterals

Cut along the dashed lines.

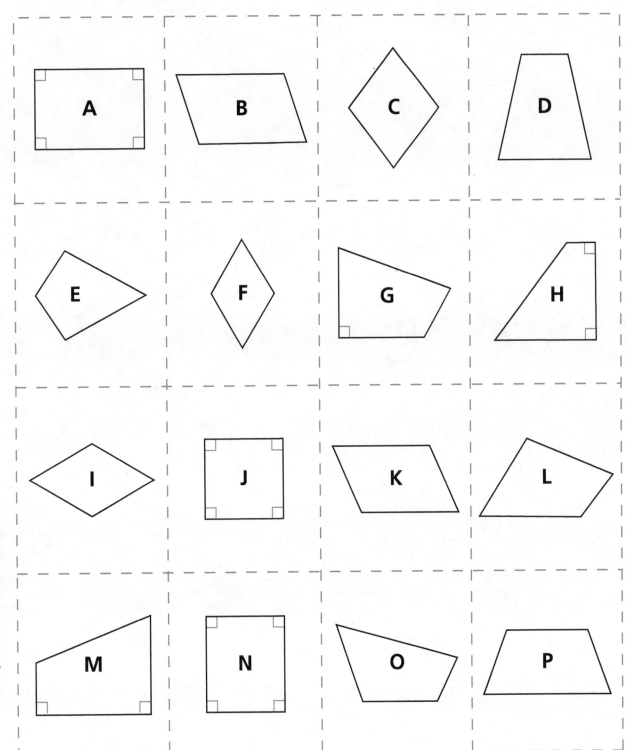

▶ Build Quadrilaterals With Triangles

You can make a quadrilateral by joining the equal sides
of two triangles that are the same size and shape.

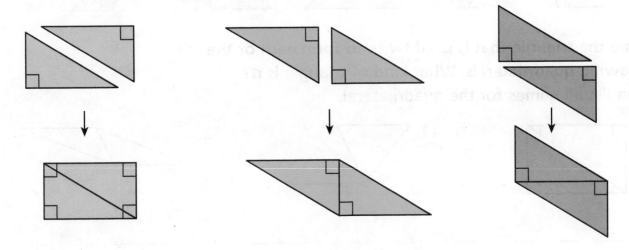

**Cut out the triangles below. For each exercise, glue two
of the triangles on this paper so that the stated sides
are joined. Then write the name of the quadrilateral.**

7. $\overline{AB}$ is joined to $\overline{AB}$ 8. $\overline{AC}$ is joined to $\overline{AC}$ 9. $\overline{BC}$ is joined to $\overline{BC}$

_____   _____   _____

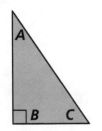
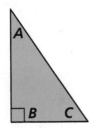
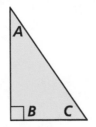
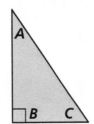
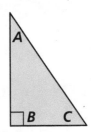
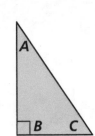

Name _____   **Date** _____

► Match Quadrilaterals with Triangles

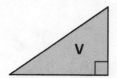 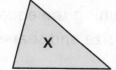

V   W   X   Y   Z

Name the triangle that is used twice to form each of the
following quadrilaterals. What kind of triangle is it?
Then list all names for the quadrilateral.

10.

_____

_____

_____

11.

_____

_____

_____

12.

_____

_____

_____

13.

_____

_____

_____

14.

_____

_____

_____

15.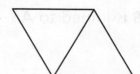

_____

_____

_____

Decompose Quadrilaterals and Triangles

▶ Sort Polygons Cards

A	**B**	**C**
D	**E**	**F**
G	**H**	**I**
J	**K**	**L**
M	**N**	**O**

Classify Polygons **137**

▶ Draw Lines of Symmetry

A line of symmetry divides a figure or design into two matching parts.

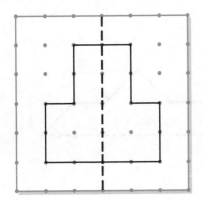   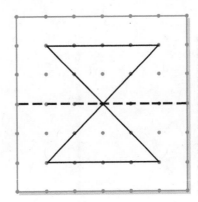

Draw the line of symmetry in the figure or design.

7.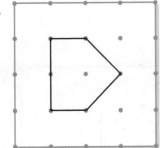

8.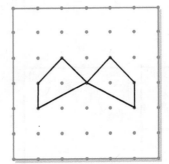

9. Which figures in Exercises 1–6 have more than one line of symmetry? _____

10. Choose one of the figures from your answer to Exercise 9. Draw the figure and draw all of its lines of symmetry.

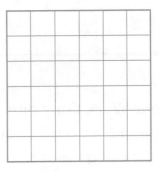

► Draw the Other Half

Draw the other half of each figure to make a whole figure or design with line symmetry.

12.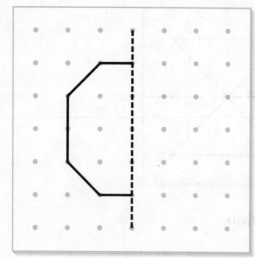

13.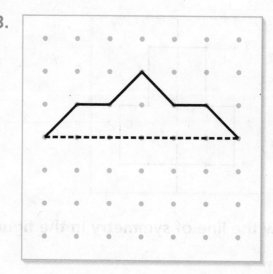

14.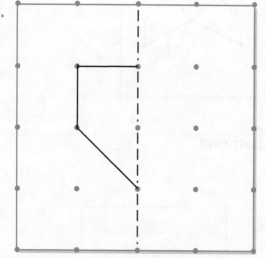

15.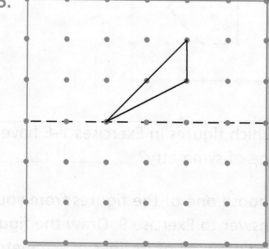

16. Check Your Work Copy one of your answers to Exercises 12–15 onto another piece of paper. Cut out the design and then fold it along the line of symmetry. Check that the two halves of the design match exactly.

Line Symmetry

1. Draw and label line segment *FG*.

2. Use a protractor to measure the angle.

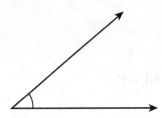

The angle measures _____.

3. Choose the figure that has at least one pair of
   parallel lines. Mark all that apply.

   Ⓐ   Ⓑ   Ⓒ   Ⓓ

4. Use the figures. For 4a–4d, select True or False for the statement.

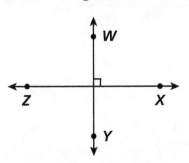 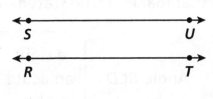

   4a. $\overleftrightarrow{ZX}$ and $\overleftrightarrow{WY}$ are parallel.   ○ True   ○ False

   4b. $\overleftrightarrow{SU}$ and $\overleftrightarrow{RT}$ are parallel.   ○ True   ○ False

   4c. $\overleftrightarrow{ZX}$ and $\overleftrightarrow{WY}$ are perpendicular.   ○ True   ○ False

   4d. A line drawn through points *R* and *U* is
       perpendicular to $\overleftrightarrow{RT}$.   ○ True   ○ False

5. The map below shows a section of Fatima's town.

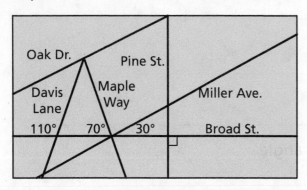

Part A

Fatima is walking on Oak Drive and Gabe is walking on Miller Ave. Could Fatima and Gabe ever meet? If so, where?

Part B

Which street is perpendicular to Broad St.? Explain how you know.

6. Choose the word that makes a true statement.

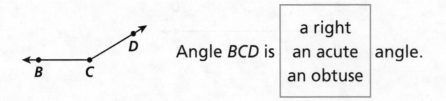

Angle *BCD* is | a right / an acute / an obtuse | angle.

7. Draw all the lines of symmetry for the figure.

8. A gear in a watch turns clockwise, in one-degree sections, a total of 300 times.

The gear has turned a total of ☐ degrees.

9. Lucy is designing a block for a quilt. She measured one of the angles. Use the numbers and symbols on the tiles to write and solve an equation to find the unknown angle measure.

| 40° | 70° | 110° | 180° | + | − |

Equation: ☐ ☐ ☐ = ?

Solution: ? = ☐

10. Luke is drawing a figure that has exactly 2 acute angles. For 10a–10d, choose Yes or No to tell if the figure could be the figure Luke is drawing.

10a. ◇ ○ Yes ○ No

10b. △ ○ Yes ○ No

10c. ☐ ○ Yes ○ No

10d. ⬠ ○ Yes ○ No

11. Triangle *QRS* can be classified

as | an acute
a right
an obtuse | triangle.

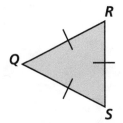

12. Choose the two angles that could be put together to make a 130° angle.

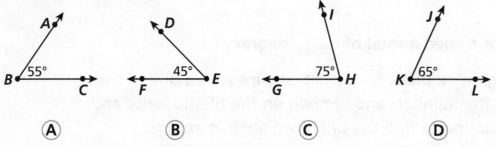

(A)   (B)   (C)   (D)

13. A sign has two pairs of parallel sides and two pairs of equal sides. What shape is the sign?

14. The circle represents all of the students in a class. Each section represents the students in the class who chose a certain color as their favorite. The angle measures for some sections are given.

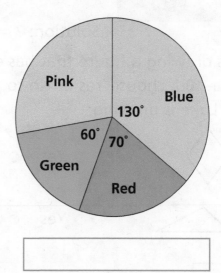

Part A

What is the sum of the angle measures for Blue, Red, and Green?

Part B

Explain how to find the angle measure for Pink. Then find the measure.

15. Draw one diagonal in the figure to form two obtuse triangles.

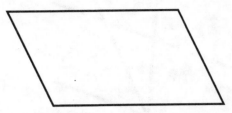

16. Does the figure have a line of symmetry? Explain.

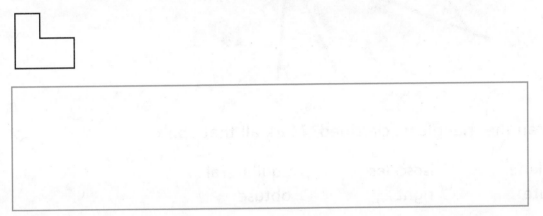

17. A Ferris wheel turns 35° before it pauses. It turns another 85° before stopping again.

Part A
What is the total measure of the angle that the Ferris wheel turned?

Part B
How many more times will it need to repeat the pattern to turn 360°?
Explain your thinking.

18. Cross Street, West Street, and Carmichael Street form a triangle.

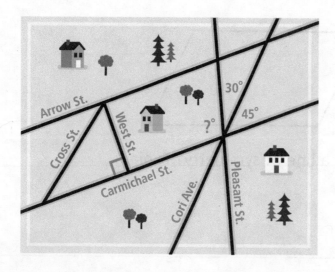

How can the triangle be classified? Mark all that apply.

○ scalene   ○ isosceles   ○ equilateral
○ acute   ○ right   ○ obtuse

19. A stage has four sides with exactly one pair of parallel sides.

Marjorie says the shape of the stage is a quadrilateral and a rectangle. Do you agree? Explain.

20. What is the unknown angle measure in this pattern?

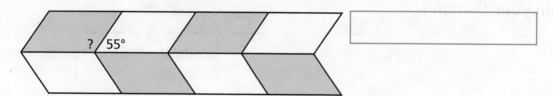

© Houghton Mifflin Harcourt Publishing Company